In easy to understand language, Todd Creager helps couples, step by step, to higher functioning in communication and sexual relating. Highly recommended for couples at all ages and stages of intimate relationship.

—Doug Moseley, co-author with wife Naomi Moseley of *The Shadow Side of Intimate Relationships* and *Making Your Second Marriage a First Class Success*

The Long, Hot Marriage is a fabulous, yet practical guide for couples that strive to work on themselves to improve their relationship. Todd Creager has a warm, personal style that can gently help readers recognize common pitfalls to having a satisfying, intimate relationship. Then he tells simply and plainly what couples can do to correct them.

—Stephanie Buehler, Psy.D. Psychologist and AASECT Certified Sex Therapist

Todd Creager has written an optimistic book filled with strategies and techniques to help couples appreciate the emotional and sexual value of a marriage which is both creative and sexual. Mr. Creager is at his best when he describes creative exercises to increase individual and couple risk-taking to break emotional and sexual impasses.

—Barry McCarthy, coauthor with wife Emily McCarthy of *Rekindling Desire- A Step-By-Step Program to Help Low-Sex and No-Sex Marriages*

Every chapter in Todd's book will have you saying, "Oh, yes, that's happened to me." The beauty about *The Long Hot Marriage* is that it doesn't slam you with boring and cold psycho-babble about why your sex life isn't working.

Todd masterfully and gently holds your hand and walks you through the maze of complicated emotions we call human sexuality. It's like having a best friend and a trained therapist to talk to you in front of a fireplace with a cup of warm cocoa. Read this book—it's fun and your sex will improve!

—Michelle Quintana, Owner of Bulldog Creative Copywriting

The Long, HOT Marriage

Todd Creager, MSW

ISBN   978-1-60013-275-9

Publishing by
INSIGHT PUBLISHING
647 Wall Street • Sevierville, Tennessee • 37862

10 9 8 7 6 5 4 3 2

ACKNOWLEDGEMENTS

Firstly, I want to acknowledge my good friend and former supervisor, Pat Carney. He got me started as a social work apprentice in my private practice in 1982 and I have cherished my relationship with him ever since. He helped shape my earliest understandings of couples and families and how people change. The way he has handled life's adversities has also been an inspiration to me.

Secondly, I want to thank all the other mentors and authors who have influenced the way I work with my clients. Special mention has to go to Judith Milburn and Doug and Naomi Moseley. Judith Milburn helped me appreciate the mysteriousness and awesomeness of our unconscious minds as well as the link between spirituality and psychology. Doug and Naomi Moseley taught me so much about how to treat couples in ways that are powerful and effective. I coordinated couples workshops for them for several years where my wife and I participated as well. They were also invaluable in helping my own marital relationship mature and thrive.

Thirdly, I want to acknowledge the people that helped me with my manuscript for this book. Chuck Kelly, my editor, is a truly talented man with the English language and helped me write some difficult to describe concepts in ways that people can more easily understand. After working with him, I have a great respect for people that are good writers. Also, my long time associate, Jan Wagniere, LCSW, gave valuable feedback. I appreciate her time and attention.

I want to acknowledge the thousands of clients through the years, whom have allowed me into their lives. I love what I do and appreciate their trust in me.

I want to acknowledge my parents, Mortimer and Dorothy Creager. My dad, who passed away four years ago, taught me about kindness to others. My mother, whose spirit and passion for life continues to soar at the age of 87, taught me that if I wanted to achieve something, I had the internal resources to do it, no matter what.

My lovely and precious daughters, Arielle and Danna have taught me so much about myself as a person and parent. Of course their biggest gift to me is the joy I feel when I am with them. I am truly blessed with them in my life.

And last but definitely not least, I want to thank my wife, Cherie. Through our 24 years of marriage we have experienced tremendous joys as well as pain. We have learned and continue to learn about what it takes to handle emotional pain more creatively and how to enjoy each other more fully. Our relationship keeps getting better and I am looking forward to our future decades together. She is a woman who is so dedicated as a wife and mother and continues to get more beautiful as time goes on.

TABLE OF CONTENTS

DISCLAIMER

H ere is my important disclaimer. Read the book and follow it. It is a roadmap to a fulfilling relationship and sexual life with your partner. However, the book should not be taken as a substitute for a skillful marriage/sex therapist. Most of us need a knowledgeable therapist to help us navigate the challenging and sometimes turbulent waters we face in a marriage. Our old habits can get in our way. We need to overcome and go beyond our old behavior patterns. To some degree, we can do this on our own. However, it may be beneficial to work with an experienced third party to help change old habits/patterns that get in the way of a successful marriage.

INTRODUCTION

"Sex and marriage are like oil and water. They just don't mix." "Look, I knew sex would decrease with kids and all the stuff we have to do every day." "I remember the days when you wanted it as much as I did." "I wish we could go back to the old days when we had sex all the time." "I guess I have to accept that we are roommates and I will have a sexless marriage." "There is no way I am staying in a sexless marriage. Do you know any good family lawyers?"

As a practicing marriage and sex therapist for over 25 years, I have heard variations on these statements thousands of times. A lack of passion in relationships seems to be the norm, for most married couples. There are of course couples that seem to go on having great and frequent sex forever. This book is for that large majority of couples that wish they could recapture the excitement of the sexual peak of their relationship. However, it is also for those couples that are having frequent, satisfying sex, because odds are their emotional and sexual relationship can still improve significantly. Also, even couples having frequent sex may feel left with a feeling of inadequacy because they are depending upon their sex life to hold their marriage together and realize that it lacks creativity and heart.

This book aims for a deeper connection that links the married couple together so that both partners continually desire each other sexually, emotionally and spiritually. This book *embraces* sexual problems as inevitable and then leads the couple to developing the attitudes, feelings and behaviors needed to be a "Full-Bodied" couple. Like full-bodied wine, a "full-bodied couple has a <u>robust</u> relationship that is rich and alive. The "full-bodied" couple stays connected through the deepest and darkest most painful moments as well as through those moments of warmth and intense pleasure.

This book is written with the sole intention of helping you discover your abilities to create a marriage that nourishes you and your partner. I have tried to make it pragmatic as well as thought provoking. The First Section is <u>The Art of Bringing the Best Out of Your Partner.</u> This section emphasizes your ability to be creative and have an impact on your partner. I put this section first on purpose. When you get out of the "victim" mentality and decide to be a positive force in your relationship, you will be able to do what the rest of the book asks of you. Section 2 is all about <u>Dealing With Pain.</u> I am convinced that most couple's dilemmas stem from the fact that most of us had parents who did not know how to deal with their own or each other's emotional pain. Fight or flight reactions rule supreme in the emotional conversations and challenges of marriage. (i.e., "I'm outa here!" instead of 'Let's talk about it.") Couples need to learn to deal with emotional pain in healthier ways; ways that lead to more rather than less connection. This is a crucial step to having more joy, sex and passion. Section 3 is <u>Sex and the Married Couple.</u> This section is probably why most people would pick up this book; the important thing to remember is that the first two sections have as much to do with having a long, hot marriage as this section. This section deals with myths of sexuality and the importance of correcting them. It talks about how to use the sexual arena of your marriage as a way to develop as a person and become more alive. It talks about the importance of "healthy dependence" and how to give as well as receive good energy, love and pleasure from others. The information in this section will definitely accelerate you along your journey toward a more passionate marriage. There are exercises throughout the book to help you practice developing the skills, mindsets and positive habits to help you achieve what has been discussed in the book.

This book focuses on several important slices of marital life and sexuality. It cannot cover the gamut of all dimensions of relationships. I did not include physical influences such as chronic illness or hormonal influences even though they all need to be considered. In my own practice, I often work closely with physicians and other health care professionals for these problems. There is a growing body of work regarding the biological side of sexuality. Drugs like Viagra and Cialis have helped men with erection problems return to sexual functioning with their wives. These erection problems could stem from physical causes such as effects of certain types of medications, certain chronic illnesses or hormonal changes and the general effects of aging. Also, when there have been psychological factors such as anxiety, Viagra and Cialis has helped these men refocus on their partners as opposed to obsessively worry about performance. I also do not talk about sex toys and aids to spice up your life. I am not at all opposed and often times will encourage such products. There are many books that are out on topics such as these. My only issue with drugs and other external supports is when the couple does not look within at the real issues/problems and too quickly depends on these aids to fix their marriage. This book helps you tap into your inner resources to have a more passionate, caring and fulfilling relationship with your spouse.

Marriage is not easy. It beckons us to grow from within and stretch our creativity and imagination to the max. If you are looking for a quick fix, this book is not for you. The ONLY way to re-sexualize marriage is 1) learn how to think about and act toward your mate with more imagination and creativity, 2) learn how to connect through both pain and pleasure and 3) discover your own sexual potential. Without developing those emotional strengths and skills, you are probably doomed to repeat the same patterns that got you where you are now. This behavior will likely continue with your current mate-- or on to your next partner.

You have something to do with the re-vitalizing of your marriage. It could perhaps be bad news because now you have to get actively involved in creating something new, something better. You cannot just sit passively and wait for your partner to be the catalyst of change. And, it could be good news because as you learn to develop those creative muscles, you can have a tremendous positive influence on your relationship.

There is reason to hope because you have undeveloped emotional capacity that when developed could lead to a great sex life with your partner. Could you imagine what could happen if each of you develop that emotional muscle? I do not have to imagine it. I have seen countless couples in my office who had given up hope, on the brink of divorce, had one or more affairs, etc., and find their way back to each other. They successfully created a connection that they never had before resulting in a vibrant, caring relationship. A lively passionate marriage is possible. Let us begin!

(The use of gender in this book is arbitrary and interchangeable unless I clearly state that written material specifically pertains to either male or female. The arbitrary use of gender helps the information flow easier without having to refer to both genders each time. The cases are actual cases from my private practice. The names and certain situations have been changed to maintain confidentiality).

SECTION 1

The Art of Bringing the Best
Out of Your Partner

1

Learning to be Creative in a Marriage

The beginning of man's time on earth was all about survival. Staying alive, capturing an animal in order to eat enough and to protect one's family was the entire focus of the human being. In time, the more fortunate ones on this planet were able to focus their time, energy and resources on other pursuits. Currently in addition to staying alive to survive, we're free to be creative in a variety of ways. This creative outlet could be through art, music, or some other hobby or avocation of choice. However, we still have those survival instincts and when called upon, can keep us alive in threatening situations.

This entire book is predicated upon an evolutionary/growth approach to couples. We are still in the very early stages of development regarding healthy long-term relationships. We respond to certain emotions and challenges as though we still have to kill the animal as in the caveman days. Since we respond to these emotional situations with fight or flight reactions, there is virtually no focus or energy left to be creative in our relationships. I optimistically believe that we are headed toward increased creativity in relationships just as we have been able to become increasingly more creative in other aspects of our lives.

What exactly is interpersonal creativity? Interpersonal creativity is any action you do, statement you make, image you think, thoughts or feelings you have that lead to something more positive between you and another person. I define 'more positive' as anything that raises the energy between two people. In other words, interpersonal creativity is positive thoughts and/or action that generate good feelings between partners in a marriage/relationship.

Energy and Good Vibrations

Modern physics teaches us that our body cells are vibrating at a particular frequency all the time. Think of yourself as a magnet that can attract positive or negative results depending upon your energy. Have you heard the expression "like attracts like?" If you ding a tuning fork in a room filled with all different kinds of tuning forks calibrated to various pitches, only the ones calibrated to the same frequency as the one you just dinged will ding too, even from far away.

As human beings we send out vibrations or energy just like a tuning fork. The difference is we can vibrate in many frequencies depending on our current emotional energy. Therefore, we can learn how to attract more of what we want out of others when we learn how to harness our energy and send out "good vibrations!" These ideas have hit the mainstream with books such as, "Ask and It Is Given" by Esther and Tom Hicks and "Excuse Me Your Life Is Waiting," by Lynn Grabhorn. Also, there is the well-known movie and book, "The Secret" that includes many people from the self-improvement field. They are all talking about "The Law of Attraction," which basically says that what we focus on is what we get. Focusing on what we don't want gets us more of what we don't want. Focusing on what we do want gets us more of what we do want. As an example, if I wanted to write this book, but I kept thinking about how I never have time to write, these thoughts could lead to feelings of frustration. With these negative thoughts, The Law of Attraction says that more obstacles will emerge to prevent me from getting the book done. However, if I focus on the finished book and how it will benefit many readers, I will find the time to write it, and probably with relative ease.

Bringing these concepts to the relationship arena is an important component of interpersonal creativity. I can ask myself before I make a statement to my partner, "Is this going to give me more or less of what I really want?" The answer to that question will help me decide whether I should say it or not. Having an interpersonally creative relationship takes work and discipline, just like painting a beautiful picture or composing a musical piece. The artist does not paint any old way, making brush strokes in a reactive, knee-jerk fashion. The musical composer does not just throw any group of notes together. Creating a beautiful painting or a pleasant melody requires some discipline, experimentation and continued modification until the artist or musician gets more of what he wants. This can be a thoroughly enjoyable process. Relating creatively to another person is no different. It also can be a thoroughly enjoyable process as we apply some discipline, experimentation and continued change.

Immediate Tension Reduction vs. Interpersonal Creativity

When couples come to see me, a common problem that is written on the intake form is "Communication." Usually, the problem has more to do with each partner's agenda or intended goal when they are trying to communicate. Three problems in communication experienced by most couples are: (1) the urge to prove oneself right (2)the need to vent and (3)defending oneself. Here is a closer look.

Proving oneself right can be very satisfying to our egos. We like to be right and we like it when people agree that we are right. It is natural for us to want to be right. It would work great if we lived in a world where our perception was always shared by everyone else. Much of what goes on between couples when in conflict is to prove the other wrong and vindicate one's own position.

Venting is often described as helpful, but it is not. Venting is only about the person venting. Venting does not take into consideration the feelings or wellbeing of the communication receiver. As graphic as it sounds, I compare this to the process of throwing up on somebody. You may feel instantly better, but the other person feels considerably worse! Venting is very tempting to do because there is an immediate tension reduction when one "throws up" his pain. Some may say that venting is good because it gets the feeling out. If as you express yourself, you are not yelling, and you are talking "to" your partner rather than "at" your partner, that is fine. I would not call that venting; I would call that sharing. Your partner is not a "sounding board." A board is two dimensional and inanimate and will not be hurt no matter how you speak your pain. As you express yourself to your partner, her wellbeing needs to be considered.

Defending oneself is a natural reaction. When someone tells us something that hurts us, we want to protect ourselves from the apparent attack just as we would if someone was shooting bullets at us. When we defend ourselves, we temporarily feel better because we are standing up for ourselves. The problem is that this automatic defense prevents us from looking at the possibility that we have been hurtful or in some ways less than perfect. It is especially difficult to look at our contribution to a problem when our partner has been hurtful to us in some way. Stagnating and destructive patterns can continue endlessly when both partners are constantly shifting from blaming the other and defending oneself from blame.

Interpersonal creativity involves communicating in such a way that when giving or receiving emotional information, the giver is able to express him/herself clearly and the receiver is not made to feel 'less than.' This is not as easy as it seems. It takes emotional muscle to redefine your communication goals. It is not natural for us to let go of the competitive way we communicate. Fear leads us to the three aforementioned ways of immediately reducing tension. It is important to see the benefits of experiencing <u>tension without trying to get rid of it too quickly.</u> As you develop the tolerance of experiencing this tension, it buys you time to be creative and learn to listen to and have empathy for the other person. Developing the tolerance of experiencing tension allows you to accept two different realities, two different ways of perceiving, wants, etc. Instead of trying to conquer the other person, you learn to coexist "as each other is." Paradoxically, the more you allow the other person to think and feel what she wants, the higher chance she just may see it more your way. Connecting like this leads to a de-escalation of pain which may then lead to a more objective outlook on things. This de-escalation needs to happen in order for the person to assimilate new information, especially if this information is somewhat painful to that person.

Courageously Getting Closer to Your Mate

The third component is about creating an interpersonal adventure. Marriage is as much of an adventure as skiing on the advanced slopes, bungee jumping or going on an African safari. The problem is that people view marriage as a haven, a place to relax, become skilled at their remote control and get a break from the stresses of work, childrearing, etc. The truth is that if you want to have a long, hot marriage you need to allow your marriage to stretch you emotionally, challenge you and get you on your edge. Your marriage needs to feel "risky" at times. There has to be a feeling of interpersonal danger on a consistent basis; then possibly cycling with periods of comfort and rest.

Relationships involve hurt and painful feelings at times. This is inevitable, and in our attempts to avoid this pain, we become increasingly distant from our partner. This distance can be felt in our bodies. The chest area feels closed and tight, the stomach area feels hardened. It is as if an armor of protection in the form of tightness and hardness is there to protect the soft stuff underneath, much like a crustacean. We need to stay open to our partners even in the heat of an argument—or when rejection of some kind is quite possible. We need to learn to soften even if our every survival instinct tells us to close down and push away. The pain we retreat from will not kill us; although retreating on a constant basis <u>will</u> kill relationships. There is no replacement for pure, unadulterated courage.

The rest of this book is all about bringing to life these three components of interpersonal creativity. Each chapter is written to help you move forward to either 1)change your energy to bring the best out of your partner, 2)become more interpersonally creative, 3)get closer to your mate—or some combination of these components.

2

Beware of Your Perceptions of

Your Partner

Everything out there is a projection because we are constantly imagining what is going on. Everything that we perceive is through our imagination. When we dream at night, every person and inanimate object in that dream is a representation of some part of who we are.

During the day we are dreaming too, because we are constantly imagining and perceiving what is going on around us. That is what we do: we have a brain—we imagine and we perceive.

In his book "The Four Agreements," Don Miguel Ruiz begins the book with a quote by John Lennon, "Living is easy with eyes closed, misunderstanding all you see…" And in the beginning of chapter 1 he writes:

"What you are seeing and hearing right now is nothing but a dream. You are dreaming right now in the moment. You are dreaming with the brain awake."

Our minds project just as a projector does in a movie theater. We project onto other people what we perceive of them. For example, if I perceive someone as a bully, I will see everything he does through the eyes of a victim. If I perceive someone as caring and giving, I will notice all the good things he says and does; I may even ignore any behavior(s) that contradict that perception.

The concept of psychological projection was originally conceived by Sigmund Freud. He describes projection as a defense mechanism in which one attributes to others one's own unacceptable or unwanted thoughts or/and emotions. In this definition, projection reduces anxiety by allowing the expression of the unwanted subconscious impulses/desires without letting the ego recognize them. I use the word "projection" in a broader sense where the perceptions we have of others is a direct result of our own brain processes, state of mind, and automatic imagination. We do not just project unwanted and unacceptable impulses out to others; everything we perceive about others is a projection. Cognitive behavioral therapy, a very effective therapy used for depression can also be useful with relationship issues based on the idea that how we think about and interpret the events around us affects our emotional state, not necessarily the events themselves. If the client can change his thoughts, he can also change how he feels even if nothing external has been altered. Likewise, we can alter the way we perceive our partner which can lead to feeling more positively towards him or her.

Our past greatly affects how we perceive of others. For example if you had a critical father growing up and your boss suddenly is annoyed with you, you may automatically project that your employer is being a critical, intimidating person like your father was, even though the boss may not be intimidating at all.

The fact that we project onto other people is not a bad thing or a good thing. It is just what we do. The trick is to become more aware of our automatic projections and then practice opening up to new perceptions. The key is to realize that our perceptions of people are not necessarily who they are. It is who we believe them to be at that moment. We are all gifted with an automatic imagination. We use this ability all the time. As long as we realize this then we are in a position to not be run by our automatic imagination. We tell ourselves imaginary stories about people all the time. If for example I am in a marriage, my experience and perception of my partner has more to do with how I am imagining this person to be than whom that person really is. That person is doing something or saying something that is stirring up something within me but how I perceive of that person has much more to do with how I'm imagining her to be.

The Importance of Forgetting History

When we are in a relationship, especially for a long period of time, we develop a pattern of interacting with each other. We start to expect things of the other person. For example, most of us are from families where we were not taught to listen, so we are not necessarily good listeners. If I come from a typical non-listening family and I am used to not being heard, I will automatically assume that my spouse is not going to listen when I talk to her. Consequently, I will probably talk to her in a way that makes it hard for her to listen because I am fighting to be heard. Maybe I raise my voice and have an edge to the way I'm talking. My partner will more than likely get on the defensive and not really listen. It becomes a self-fulfilling prophecy. We do this dance together, where I have an edge to my voice and she does not listen. The result is always the same—no listening. And I believe that she is a poor listener and I feel sorry for myself!

The problem is just that: it repeats itself until it becomes history. It has nothing to do with the potential of the partner. This repetitious routine distorts our perception and clouds our ability to perceive what the potential of one's partner really is as a true listener.

Of course, there are memories we cherish and we use photographs and DVD's to remember precious moments. History has its place in our family and marital lives. What is being discussed here is that some history does need forgetting. That means that we cannot afford to let history run us. Negative patterns from the past can stay alive and well in the present if we assume history will repeat itself.

You Treat People According To How You Perceive Them

And They In Turn Act According To How You Treat Them.

In other words if I perceive you as a poor listener, I will treat you accordingly, i.e., I will treat you as someone who will not listen to me. I will have an edge, I might raise my voice, or I may just retreat from you. I perceive of you as a non-listener so I push you away.

We treat people the way we perceive them. We start treating them as though they do not listen to us and of course after awhile it becomes a self-fulfilling prophecy.

There are many, many examples of this in marriages. Another example involves distrust. Let's say you come from a family where your father cheated on your mother. In addition, your first husband cheated on you as well. You are now married again and in the back of your mind, you are worried that he will cheat on you one day. You get angry whenever he goes on a business trip and you interrogate him every night, being hyper-vigilante about how much alcohol he has had. He may have no plans whatsoever to cheat on you and may drink responsibly; however, he is getting increasingly resentful that you are mothering and smothering him. You are pushing him away and increasing the chances that whether by an affair or some other means, he will *prove to you once again that men are not to be trusted.* You can easily see the self-fulfilling prophecy working here. In this example, it would be important for you to challenge your own automatic perceptions and believe in your own power to be a positive influence on your partner.

When I was in my first year of graduate school I was in an inpatient unit working with severely depressed people. My ambition was to work as a therapist in an outpatient setting with people who were more functional. I made sure I got that kind of placement in my second year. I had never had outpatient experience; it was brand new to me. The year before I had a wonderful relationship with two supervisors; we had a good time, I learned a lot and they thought well of me. When I met my second year supervisor, before the semester even started, I remember walking to my car saying to myself, "Wow, did you feel the chill in the air!" I knew that she didn't like me and I didn't know why. There was no way she could judge me on merit because the semester hadn't even started.

When the semester began she continued to show that she was not very fond of me. Within a week she told me she didn't believe that I was ready to graduate with my class. According to her I was not on par with some of the other students.

I reminded her that I had just started and said, "I can't understand why you are thinking this way." However, she was a much respected person; the psychiatrists liked and respected her and other experienced clinicians went to her for advice and consultations. I started to wonder that maybe she was right and I really wouldn't be ready to graduate with my class as she had repeated several times. My confidence went down. My therapy skills were below par and my clients were not improving. I continued to do worse and worse until finally by December, I wrote her a letter stating that I quit. I couldn't do this any more. When I handed her the letter, she gave me a letter firing me on the same day I was quitting!

Luckily for me I soon got another field placement. I met my new supervisor and it felt like I had returned home. I could feel and see right away that the new supervisor welcomed me and it became a great semester. Most of my clients improved greatly, and consequently referred other people to the agency to see me. In April, my supervisor approached me and said that she went to USC and had seen the evaluation this other supervisor wrote about me. "Who is this person that she wrote about? It is not the person I know," my supervisor said. I replied, "It was that other supervisor's perception of me." From her recommendation the counseling agency hired me right out of graduate school to continue working with them.

I went from being this person who was "not ready to graduate with my class" to someone who did well enough that the agency hired me on my merits. As you can see my performance was significantly affected by the perceptions of the two supervisors, both in a negative and a positive way.

That is a personal example of how we often act according to how people treat us—and how they treat us is affected by how we are perceived.

Examples of Negative Perceptions That Lead To Self-Fulfilling Prophecies

My partner is a poor listener.
My partner cannot handle money.
My partner will cheat on me.
My partner is too serious.
My partner is too controlling.
My partner is too soft.
My partner is sexually inhibited.
My partner does not express his feelings.
My partner is self-absorbed.
My partner is immature.

The comments could go on and on, of course. The above list contains the most common perceptions/beliefs I hear in my office that ultimately limit relationships and keep them from growing.

Most People Are Changeable.

People tend to view not only themselves but other people as if they are their "fixed patterns of behavior." They identify themselves and others with their behavior history. The truth is, based on our past environments; we all have developed patterns of speaking, acting, feeling, imagining, and thinking. If we change the current environment then we increase the possibilities for ourselves and our partners to develop new ways of speaking, acting, feeling, imagining, and thinking. People are basically more malleable than we realize. We are like clay before it hardens. We can learn new patterns. We do not know what people's potentials are as partners, mates or in other arenas like work. If we have this idea that people are changeable; that they have the ability to grow beyond themselves, then we will treat them differently instead of seeing them as fixed entities.

It is vitally important to see people as malleable. It is probably one of the most important beliefs to cultivate for a long, hot marriage. When a couple comes to see me for therapy, one of the first things I do is give them hope. One of the ways I do that is to tell or remind them that people are capable of acting in healthier, more constructive ways even if history shows that they have been stuck in old behavior patterns. What I do as a therapist is to help them create an environment that allows for this flexibility to come into being.

Don't Wait To Perceive Your Partner Differently. Do It

NOW!

We need to recognize immediately that our perception of our partner plays a large part in what goes on in the relationship. Ask yourself, "What is my automatic perception of my partner?"

An example of a couple I treated who learned to work with automatic perceptions was Tom and Mary. Mary was overly-involved with her children, leaving her husband to feel that he was being pushed out. The more I explored her behavior I realized that this was her safety net. She felt safe around her kids. Since her husband was often critical of her, she perceived him as someone who was emotionally dangerous. He was a successful and powerful man—and she felt unworthy around him. I ask her how she felt when he comes home and she hears him walking towards the front door. She said that she would immediately get butterflies in her stomach and wanted to run away. I told her that when she started to have that feeling, to say to herself- "Instead of perceiving my partner as a scary person, I'm going to perceive him as a person who has his own feelings and opinions but is <u>not</u> dangerous." Then she was to ask herself how she would act towards him when she perceived him in this new way.

The first day after the session she did talk to herself as we discussed when she heard him walk towards the front door. When he walked in, instead of running to her children she told him how she felt. She told him about the butterflies in her stomach and how she wanted to run away. She said that she knew the butterflies in her stomach were part of an automatic reaction to him. The fact that she was expressing her true feelings to him already was indicative of a person who trusted her husband enough to be vulnerable. In other words, she was treating him as if he was safe by the very action of expressing her fear of him. Running to the children would have given more power to her belief that he was "scary". By expressing herself directly gave strength to her new belief that he was a caring, loving husband, and safe to be around. His reaction was perfect! He said, "Thank goodness you are talking to me. I am sorry you had to feel that way." Then he gave her a hug and that was the beginning of shifting that behavior pattern.

The sooner we begin perceiving our partner differently, the sooner we will get results. It may not always be as immediate as the above but I encourage people to believe in the power of their perceptions. We tend to say that we will change our perceptions when our partner's behavior changes. What I am doing is turning the order around. Instead of waiting for the behavior to change so that the perception will change, alter the perception to a more positive one even before there is any history of the positive behavior. And then you will see how the new perception affects you especially in the long term.

Experiment with New Perceptions

Give yourself permission to experiment with new perceptions. It is important to look at these experiments in the following way: We have the ability to be creative, including being interpersonally creative. Think of a musician who is creating a musical piece or an artist who creates a painting.

They don't wait for the picture to appear or the music to sound. They do something about it.

I have been playing the accordion since I was 7 years old. (No accordion jokes please!) I read the musical notes and play songs. Recently, I started to study jazz and blues improvisation. After learning some basic blues and jazz scales, I began to experiment with new melodies. Creating my own music is a wonderfully freeing process. I still enjoy looking at notes and playing structured melodies, but to have the knowledge to experiment with new melodies and not be restricted is very different and pleasurable, not to mention it is highly creative. After I learned the basic scales, I was able to make the melodies happen based upon choosing what notes to play; and the choices are endless. Likewise, once you figure out the positive perceptions you need to cultivate of your partner, you can choose from an endless number of statements and behaviors that will support the positive beliefs you are cultivating. Interpersonal creativity means you make something happen between the two of you and it often takes courage; more courage than it takes to be a jazz accordionist. The reason for the initial fear is that there is a big unknown. How will my partner react to this new and original perception/behavior? I have been told by artists and musicians how scary it is for them to let other people see or hear their work. It is their creation and they are not sure how people will react. It is even more threatening when it is your partner whom you hope will accept you and treat you well. When we do the automatic perception along with the automatic behavior it is typically a way to protect ourselves from some imaginary harm we feel that may happen to us. The case of Tom and Mary illustrates this. For years Mary let her fear push her to avoid her husband and to become over-involved with her children. This is a very passive way of being. It is the opposite of being creative. Creativity and passivity are opposites. Creativity starts with the idea that 'I have something to do with the problem so therefore I have something I can do to create a solution.' This involves risk; it involves putting yourself out there and not going along with one's automatic behavior.

I cannot emphasize enough the importance of treating conversations, touching, and other ways of connecting as experiments. The relationship becomes comprised of a series of interpersonal experiments of perceptions and behavior. This is SO DIFFERENT from the typical way we look at relationships. Relationships are not meant to be havens from the stress of everyday life. In between trying on new perceptions and trying out new behaviors, you can definitely rest, but let the respite be temporary. Creativity in relationships is an ongoing process. A person's perceptions are very powerful and they have a huge effect on their relationship. It is vitally important to experiment, try out new things and see what results you get. A person who is good at experimenting does not give up right away. He is persistent even when the other person may not initially react well to the new behavior(s). David Schnarch, author of "Passionate Marriage" and "Resurrecting Sex," says (in Resurrecting Sex) that on average a person needs to experiment with new behaviors six times before he gets a positive result from his partner. At first, the partner may be running to protect herself and act in old self-protective ways. Persistence, courage and faith will be worth your while as you get more of what you want from your mate.

The Power of Positive Perception Eventually Evokes the Desired Behavior (most of the time).

There are people with personality disorders and other psychological limits who are truly stuck. A person with a personality disorder may never be able to treat you the way you deserve to be treated. However, for the most part, when we make believe that our spouses are absolutely wonderful we act differently towards them and we bring out the best in them. We need to make this our belief. What is a belief? A belief is basically an idea that we have given much thought and put energy into. Usually the beliefs that we have are automatic that were created to make sense of our world as a child or to protect ourselves from danger(s). We believe that something out there that is threatening us. In other words, the belief had a reason. The problem is that our automatic beliefs usually come at a cost. Part of the problem is that we are self protective. We protect ourselves most of the time. If you perceive your partner as someone who is going to disappoint you then you will not be as disappointed as much as if you expected more. If you are walking up a ladder and you fall on the second rung, you will not get hurt as much as if you fall from the seventh rung of the ladder. If I have been hurt before whether it was from my present partner, a past partner, a parent, or other caretaker, my automatic reaction will be to avoid being disappointed, let down or hurt. My coping mechanism will be to proceed with caution. In other words I would not see you as wonderful, because I may get hurt more. In order to see you as wonderful, I need to be willing to get hurt again and not play it safe. We will talk more about being open and courageous in a later chapter. Just remember that it all starts with experimenting with new perceptions so that you can begin an upward spiral in your relationship.

What an upward spiral would look like

You immerse yourself in the perception that your wife is wonderful. You remember times in the past that you truly experienced her that way. You look beyond the problems and imagine her to be a person becoming more loving, more (fill in the blank) than she has ever been. You look at her imperfections as just making her human. You remember all the best attributes about her. You see her "less than desirable" patterns as temporary and see her as capable of changing those patterns. Since you perceive her more positively than your old, automatic way, you smile at her more. You look at her differently since you see her as caring and loving towards you, even though she possibly has not shown it recently. Your tone is gentle and loving as if you believed she was going to listen to you. Instead of harsh eyes, you have soft eyes, even though you were possibly frustrated with each other just a few moments ago. She seems to still be upset, but her

17

anger shifts to sadness and then possibly tears. She suddenly comes and hugs you and expresses her pain to you, but this time she is more vulnerable. There is no attack in her tone of voice. At this moment you are now in a place where some real healing, connecting, and growth can take place. In Section 2, you will learn to deal with emotional pain more constructively. Shifting perceptions sets the stage for the adult-to-adult interactions described in Section 2. Shifting perceptions is also the most powerful way to quickly shift a relationship from painful to pleasurable. We all have a need to feel close; and yet we are terrified of it. Shifting to more positive perceptions creates an atmosphere of safety where getting close becomes easier.

Personal Example

I came from a family where my parents fought a lot and were often unhappy with each other. I learned at an early age that if I did wonderfully at school, behaved myself and was an overall "good boy," it gave my parents something to be happy about. Pleasing others had immediate rewards as I received praise and recognition. The unconscious goal was to make sure everyone around me was satisfied.

I have been married 24 years. In my marital relationship, I had a hard time standing up for myself since my unconscious goal was still to "please the other." For the first part of my marriage, I perceived my wife as restricting and unyielding. At some point I understood that my perceptions of her were clouding the truth as well as limiting the relationship. I asked myself, "How would I react to her if I perceived her as a person who was flexible?" Perhaps I had not even given her a chance. If I perceived her as flexible then I would be asking more of what I needed from her. I decided to give her many more opportunities to be flexible. And here is the interesting thing I learned: She is flexible! Sometimes she does not like what I want to do. Sometimes she may not be happy with what I suggest, but to a point she will go along with it. Sometimes I yield, sometimes she yields. She is not a restricting person. However, she is a person that may differ in her feelings, preferences or desires. When we are dealing with something we don't agree on, that is all it is, a disagreement. When I perceive her more positively, I speak to her and look at her differently. That makes all the difference.

Patterns can change and change begins with you. Of course it takes two to tango, but do not wait for your partner to initiate change. Start experimenting with new perceptions. Imagine your partner as an absolutely wonderful spouse. My experience with thousands of couples, including my own relationship, is that when seeing him in a different way (despite your history together); this new perception will bring out another side to your partner.

Exercises to Bring the Best Out of Your Partner ☺

Imagine your partner to have more of the traits that you wish for. How would you talk to her? How would you look at her? What would you ask of her? How would you touch her? Then experiment with talking, looking, asking, and touching her as you visualized.

Ask yourself, "What do I need to bring out of myself that is new and different that would make it easier for my partner to be more of what I want her to be? For example, if you want your partner to be more accepting, maybe you need to be a better listener. You can become that listening person. See how that affects the behavior of your partner.

If your relationship is stuck in a rut where there is distance and/or resentment, announce to her that you have been stuck in a rut. Tell her that you forgot how beautiful, wonderful…she is because of how you have been feeling. Demonstrate your love through an embrace or gentle touch. Do not wait to "feel" like doing this. And definitely do not wait for your partner to perceive you differently or treat you better.

Be willing to surprise your partner with your new creative behavior. Tolerate the tension that you may experience when she does not trust your new behavior just yet. Reassure her that this is the real you; you just have to show it more consistently and that she will trust and enjoy it more as time goes on. (Don't always expect instant applause).

3

High Impact Partners

No matter what I do, it is never enough for her." Do you ever feel that way? Do you get frustrated feeling that you can never please your partner? Do you see yourself as a spouse who contributes greatly to the household, family, finances, etc. but your partner seems to only focus on the negative? Many partners experience that kind of frustration. It would be easy to categorize the unsatisfied partner as difficult to please, ungrateful and/or moody. However, there may be another reason for her displeasure and there may be a relatively simple solution to her disappointment and your frustration.

Giving from Your Weakest Link

High impact partnering is when a partner does or says things that uplift the energy of his partner in a big way. The high impact partner does and says the things that have the most leverage to have the most significant positive effect on his mate. Ask yourself, "What makes my partner tick? What does she like? What is the one thing my partner needs from me, that if I gave that to her, she would be elated?" You could be giving in all kinds of ways but if what you are doing is not what is essential to her emotional well being, it is not going to give you what you want. It is natural for you to give in ways that come easy for you. For example, you may be a very handy person and you can fix things around the house, build furniture and do other projects that improve your family's living situation. In addition, maybe you help with the kids, bring home a good paycheck, and sometimes wash the dishes! Meanwhile, you have a wife who more than anything wants to feel emotionally close to you. She wants to learn more about how you feel, what you want and what your dreams are. She also wants you to show interest in what she is experiencing. She would love to have you ask her questions that allow her to express herself to you. Despite all your giving, she may be unsatisfied if you do not spend the time and energy to attend to her emotional needs for closeness. With high impact partnering you are going to ask what the core needs of your partner are. You may have to stretch outside your comfort zone to meet her needs. Giving your attention to her feelings as well as expressing your own may not be a natural skill you have. It often takes giving from a less developed aspect of yourself to be that high impact partner.

Curiosity

You need to get curious about your partner's needs. What makes your partner feel alive? What thrills his or her soul? What motivates your partner? You need to apply those questions to yourself as well. Your answers to these questions can become guideposts to making decisions to creating a lifestyle that benefits both of you. Your answers can help you plan the days of your life to make sure you experience those things that evoke your enthusiasm as well as that of your mate. In order to have a "Long, Hot Marriage," each person needs to have an emotional spark; that feeling of joy to be alive and a high level of energy to devote to one another. As part of a couple, it would behoove you to help find your spark as well as that of your partner.

Examples of High Impact Partnering

Ted and Lori were married with a 13 year old daughter. Ted was an electrician and owner of a small but successful company. His wife was the office manager and accountant. Ted was great at managing crises whether it was technical or interpersonal. Sometimes, the way he solved problems did not take into account that he was possibly setting up some bad precedent for the future. In his home life he also lived in the present, sometimes eating too much, drinking too much, and looking forward to sex with his wife. His wife was turned off by his overweight body and his excessive eating and drinking habits. Lori was an attractive, energetic women who thrived on organization and feeling a sense of progress. This need for "progress" was experienced both at work and home. Her face would light up whenever she talked about some improvement she made at work, or when her daughter accomplished something significant or when her husband handled a challenge at work with poise and skill. Sexually, she felt that because he was out of shape, they were not enjoying sex as much as they could. At work, she was frustrated because despite his great skill as an adaptable crisis manager, she did not see him doing things that would eventually help the business to grow. He was angry because of her constant negative feedback and his inability to please her sexually as well as in other areas.

In therapy, each partner began to understand each others core needs. They softened their perceptions. Instead of Tim seeing her as non-accepting and controlling, he understood her need for progress and mastery. Instead of resisting her, he now was motivated to develop healthier eating habits. He drank less and exercised more which led to his having more confidence and a greater ability to enjoy sex. His willingness to "make progress" in his health had tremendous positive impact on her. She even found herself overlooking some of the less important irritants. She was able to appreciate his desire for excitement and fun and made it a point to be more fun herself!

At work, they both learned to appreciate each other's complementary strengths. He realized that even though he had to focus on the present, he needed to have one eye on the future as well and see the big picture. This was not a natural process for him; if left to his automatic habits, he would not even think about the future implications of his way of handling work challenges. Lori needed to let go to some degree of her need to have things in perfect order. She understood that if her husband had to always check himself and not be spontaneous that would deplete his energies. She saw his need for freedom and spontaneity as a valid need rather than an obstacle to her need for constant maximum progress and ideal strategy.

Ted and Lori recognized the core needs in each other and stretched themselves to give each other as much of what each needed to thrive. This stretching has to be done consciously and consistently. They had their occasional setbacks as we all do. He would start to see her as too controlling and she would start to see him as too impulsive. The good news for this couple is they were able to shift out of their power struggles and come back to this central principle of high impact partnering.

Paying Attention to What Elevates Your Partner's Energy

Here is a great question to ask your partner. "What would you like to do if you had the opportunity that would make you feel more alive?" You need to know what makes your partner feel glad to be alive and to encourage those behaviors. It becomes obvious that there are two winners when you do this; she wins because she gets to feel alive and passionate and you benefit because when she feels this way, chances are she will give you more positive attention as well.

My wife loves to go Israeli Folk Dancing. I like it too, but it is a struggle for me since it can be challenging and I am not as coordinated as she. I encouraged her to go every week to the dance class even though a part of me would have loved her to stay home so that I would not be the only one having to deal with the kids' homework, bedtime, etc. When she returned home from dancing, she would be in a wonderful mood and treated me as if I was the husband of the year.

When I work with couples I sometimes say that if one partner is having it too much his way then the other is possibly being too accommodating. Ultimately both partners lose out when this happens. If you have a partner that is too accommodating and is not doing the things that makes her tick ultimately her level of aliveness decreases. A person at a high level of aliveness is joyful, passionate and enthusiastic. A person at a low level of aliveness is depressed and/or apathetic. There is a continuum between these two extremes. At a lower level of aliveness, she is not going to want to have sex with you because she is not going to be motivated, or she is too tired. Sometimes it takes sacrifice on one person's part to encourage the level of aliveness in the other, just as I did when my wife went Israeli folk dancing. There has to be a constant give and take between two people.

These are some possible questions to ask yourself AND your partner:

- What are the types of people you need to be around who make you tick?
- Do you need to be alone at times?
- Do you need to be around more people?
- What am I not doing or saying to you as a spouse that if I did, would make your day?
- What are your dreams?
- Do you have a secret fantasy?
- Are you passionate about your job? If not, what kind of job would you like to have?
- If we could arrange our lifestyle differently that would suit you better, what would that be?

Of course this is a small sample of questions, but I am sure you get the idea. Be constantly aware of what makes your partner tick.

Bob and Nancy

Nancy was very frustrated with her husband. They had some major issues with their oldest son. The son, now approaching his mid- 20's was still at home, not trying to get a job or going to school and sponging off his parents. Nancy wanted Bob to finally put his foot down and give their son the ultimatum- "Find a job and start paying rent within a month or you are out of the house." Bob did follow through with making that statement to their son. Bob had been a passive parent who did not set boundaries with his children. The house was run by the kids, an upside down situation that happens in homes where parents do not give structure and give in to children's impulses in order to keep the peace. He was trying hard to change some of his parenting styles; not only with the older son but with all three children. Despite his progress in his parenting, his wife was still frustrated. She often had a sour look on her face and Bob was getting more and more discouraged. He was ready to give up.

I realized that Nancy was always needing to manage and oversee things and taking on too much of the masculine role. What she really needed was to feel feminine; feel a sense of, "My partner is being strong for me and being there for me." Even though he was making progress as a parent, he was *responding to her direction* and he needed to be more of an *initiator and give Nancy a chance to respond to him.* During one session, I said to him, "I want you to make an impact on Nancy right now in this session. What can you do right now that would make her feel a sense of hope, a sense of femininity and give her other good feelings?" He looked at me and we stared at each other for a minute or two but I did not say anything. After a few moments, he took her into his arms and he gave her a mad passionate kiss on the lips. She was surprised and you could see her whole attitude was different. I asked, "Was this the kind of thing he does at home?" She said, "Never." This self-initiated act was definitely different.

What he did in my office had nothing to do with parenting, or with him being more cooperative; it had to do with him being a leader in the interaction and giving his wife a chance to receive and respond to him. She totally softened and they walked out hand in hand. This shift of emotion between them continued throughout the month their son was still living with them. The son did not look for a job and was kicked out of the house. The significant point is: as important as it was to follow through with the son, the behavior that had the major impact was the husband's ability to initiate and evoke new feelings in his wife. He did something spontaneous—and she liked it.

Declare that you will be a High Impact Partner. Ask yourself, "What is something that is really difficult for me to do that if I did it, there would be a good chance it would make a positive impact on my partner?" Asking this question will often lead you to come up with spontaneous ideas. Sometimes, these ideas, if followed through require you to tolerate some anxiety or discomfort if it is not a natural behavior. Be willing to tolerate some anxiety to get the benefits of being a High Impact Partner.

Examples from my Practice

1. The "logical, thinking" husband devotes 10 minutes minimum per day to sharing and listening with his "feelings-oriented" wife.

2. The sexually conservative wife surprises her husband with a sexy strip-tease.

3. The husband who drinks too much goes to AA and demonstrates a willingness to "clean up his life."

4. The wife who spent money to feel good chooses to get therapy and live within the family budget.

5. The overly serious husband pulls his wife off the couch and dances with her in his living room.

6. The wife who can be overly critical starts a new habit of telling her husband the things she appreciates about him.

You may see yourself in one or more of these scenarios or maybe you can think of your own scenario where you and/or your partner are giving but not in the highest impact area. You can probably imagine the impact of these kinds of behavioral changes. As you discover your highest leverage actions, you can look forward to the transformative power of your new behaviors that can instantly raise the energy inside of your partner and the aliveness in the relationship.

SECTION 2

Dealing with Pain

4

Developing Emotional Muscle

The Problem with Reactivity

When I see couples that are facing challenges, as we all do, it really comes down to one thing: We haven't witnessed our relatives or ancestors deal with pain in a healthy way. Our parents and grandparents didn't really show us any good constructive ways to deal with pain. What we saw were couples reacting to each other. The reacting could come in one or two different ways: It could be a 1) fight reaction or a 2) flight reaction. Fight or flight is the most common way to deal with a perceived threat. But most of the time, the perceived threat is an illusion-- an illusion that keeps the couple disconnected.

Should your partner express a negative feeling to you, and you react defensively, you have probably made it worse. Since you have not considered what she was feeling, your partner is more than likely angrier than she was before. The more we react, the more negative will be the consequences from our reactions. It then becomes a negative spiral. It also keeps the relationship shallow because there is always more to our partner behind the original comment that upset us in the first place. A negative reaction doesn't allow for a deeper knowing of the other person.

The 10th day of the 6th month

There was a study done some time ago that found that the median age of a couple falling out of love was the 10th day of the 6th month of a relationship. You could say facetiously that on the 9th day of the 6th month pain has not emerged much at all. When we as a couple first get together everything is wonderful! We are IN LOVE and see only the positive. If negativity rears its ugly head we shove it away because we don't want anything to interfere with this wonderful moment we are having with our partner. Everything is all bliss and happiness. But at some point reality emerges and we painfully realize we aren't perfect. We were not born to constantly please anyone, including our mate, so we ultimately evoke pain in each other at least by the 10th day of the 6th month. Of course for some couples it could be much earlier, and later for others. When that pain appears for the first time, we haven't a clue how to deal with this behavior. Typically a person will try to hide it; to suppress it; he doesn't want to ruin the moment. On the other hand, the person may handle it in a reactive way to reduce his tension.

Having a game of emotional catch

When your partner expresses pain, you probably have pain also. The way you may deal with pain is oftentimes reactive so there is no giving and taking. Think of an actual game of "catch" with your partner. You throw the ball to her. If she catches it, then it is agreeable. But if you throw the ball and she just watches it hit the ground, it is very frustrating. We have to learn how to "catch" feelings in the same way. If she throws you a feeling or perception, your job is to "catch" it. You have to take it in before you throw it back to her. Our parents and grandparents did not do this. What we typically observed was one person either defending oneself or debating with the partner. That is why I always say to marital partners not to be hard on themselves or each other for having problems. Problems with communication and connection are inevitable. There are lots of things to be stressed and emotional about. Remember not to beat yourself up, or judge your partner unnecessarily. Instead, ask how can I go forward and learn from this experience? How can I learn to evolve so that I can deal with pain so that it does not take over our relationship?

Developing the Listening Muscle

Working out does not produce muscles; we have muscles already. However, if a person wants to be stronger, he has to work out to develop those muscles and make them more prominent. Similarly, we have inside of us the ability to listen. It is underdeveloped. It is easy to listen to people when they are talking about non-threatening subjects such as the weather. Most, if not all of us, do not have a well developed listening muscle when it comes to negative feedback. We tend to give into what ever feeling that person is provoking in us and we react to the inner feeling rather than listening. Listening occurs when the person who is expressing has the subjective experience of feeling that the partner opened up to receiving the feeling (just like catching the ball). If my partner expresses something and I react in a way that leaves her feeling that she has not been listened to, then I wasn't listening in the first place, even when I thought I was. You cannot be listening if the expressing person does not experience that you are. The art of listening takes a lot of work. We have to learn to develop our listening muscle.

When it comes to developing your listening skills, marriage is the weight room. Where an actual weight room has barbells and machines to challenge you physically, marriage challenges you emotionally because your pain gets brought into being more than in any other relationship. This is primarily due to the intimate nature of the marital bond and the expectations and needs we have of each other. Under the sometimes challenging nature of marriage, we need to learn how to calm our body and minds in order to listen to an emotional spouse. We cannot afford to act on our own discomfort when our partner is expressing something that is important to her. When we react in this way, we are definitely 'dropping the ball' in our own court.

First it is important that you learn relaxation exercises. You need to learn how to take breath into your diaphragm and then exhale. Practice breathing deeply, relaxing your muscles and accepting yourself. Sometimes your partner will not like you or something you said or did. Your partner may judge or criticize you. At these times, I would assert that it is your responsibility to soothe yourself and accept your own worthiness in the midst of her judgment. Breathing deeply helps you stay centered so that you may listen in these challenging circumstances.

The second thing you need to do is to get out of your own way. Focus your attention on your partner and her emotional needs instead of your own stuff. Move out of your own orbit, (your own thinking, feelings, etc.) which is so easy to get stuck in. Instead, when you are feeling uncomfortable or even disagreeing with what your partner is saying, focus on what is going on with her. Try to imagine what she is experiencing right now. Allow your partner's experience and feelings to take center stage. What you are feeling is incidental now and can be put on the backburner to be dealt with later.

The third thing to do is some kind of outward gesture whether it is saying "yes" or repeating her words to let her know that you are not only here physically but you are here emotionally with her. You are listening to what she is saying. Acknowledging her words with a nod can be an effective way to let your partner know that you are tuning in to her (as long as you do it in a sincere way as opposed to a rote, mechanical way.) This kind of listening is similar to being a good journalist. An excellent journalist will try to get as much information out of a person as possible, and he does so by asking open ended questions and by putting all his attention on the person he is interviewing. He also double checks the information to find out if his perceptions of what you are saying are correct. He wants the person he interviewed to wake up the next morning, read the story about him in the paper and say, "Yes, he got the story exactly right! He really understood what I said to him!" A listener who is developing his listening muscle is also learning to ask open ended questions. He is curious and asks his partner to tell him more, giving some outward gesture that he is tuning in and making sure he understands her.

I give couples listening workouts in my office. We pick an emotionally charged subject and, the rules are, they need to listen to each other. If either partner gets on the defensive, I block that response and have the partner go through the steps:

1) Self-soothe. Breathe into your diaphragm and exhale all the way out. Do this as many times as it takes to get calm. Remind yourself that you are worthy and adequate.

2) Refocus your attention on your partner and what he is expressing to you.

3) Give him some verbal and/or non-verbal indication that you are listening.

Once she is back on track and doing the above steps, I ask her to bring more information out of him by asking questions. This is hard to do because there is a big part of her that does not want to listen to this, especially if it evokes uncomfortable feelings in her. After this exercise is done and there are more exchanges, I ask her to summarize what she thinks he is experiencing or feeling. If he lets her know that she listened, she can choose to have a turn. If not, they have as many exchanges as needed to get to a point of understanding and rapport. Then it is his time to be the listener. I take him through the above steps in the same way.

Home assignments are given so that the couple can practice listening to each other. You, the reader, may or may not have the benefits of a third person, such as a therapist keeping you on track. If you do not have that luxury (sometimes it is a necessity), be kind and patient with each other as you go through the exercises. Check your ego at the door when you do this exercise. Otherwise, it could turn into a debate.

Sometimes people may feel it is structured and mechanical but it is helpful to have a set of instructions to follow in the beginning when you are developing new listening muscle. The following subsection is important to be successful with this exercise.

Developing The Constructive Expression Muscle

Ask yourself, how can I express myself to make it easier for others to listen? We have to understand that listening is a very difficult thing to do. Unfortunately our ancestors did not always teach us how to listen. The person speaking must express herself in ways that make it easier for the listener to stay connected and not to get on the defensive.

First, you want to make "I" statements. If you have learned anything on healthy communication, you have learned this basic and absolutely essential concept. Start out with "I feel sad," or "I feel angry," and so on, expressing how you feel. This is to reveal something about yourself. After saying the sentence, you will feel a little more vulnerable than you did before. It is common for people to say "I feel" followed by the word "that". When you say "I feel that" you are probably going to reveal a thought or judgment. An example is- "I feel that you are a bad listener," instead of "I feel hurt because you are not listening to me." The second way promotes some understanding and reveals how the expresser feels. Another example of an "I" statement is "I am disappointed when you seem to disregard what I'm saying," or "I feel angry when you do this," or "What I really want from you is to put down the newspaper and look at me in the eyes when I speak with you." These are "I" statements.

The first rule then is "I" statements and no "you" statements because "you" statements typically lead to some kind of judgment and criticism that will make it easier for the other person to get on the defensive.

The second thing is to imagine your partner as a good listener even if past experience dictates otherwise. Before you even say a word catch yourself and notice if your automatic perception is that your partner is going to be reacting and not caring. Make a conscious perception that your partner is capable of listening to you.

The third helpful way of being a constructive conversationalist/ communicator is, 'before expressing a negative thought,' you may want to throw in a positive thought first. Let us say that your partner is being inattentive or tuning you out. You could say, "I know that you have been working on listening to me and I really appreciate that, but the last few days you seem to have gone backwards and I'm feeling a little sad about that," which would be an effective way of expressing yourself. Or you could say, "I know that you have had a tough time at work lately and I can appreciate that, but I still need for you to listen to me." Here, you are giving your partner some sense of understanding. This attitude will hopefully lead to less defensiveness and a higher probability of communication between you both.

The Importance of Body Awareness

As you read these words, pay attention to how your abdominal area feels. Is it relaxed or tight? Now notice how your jaw area feels. Is it clenched or relaxed? If you are sitting, notice the sensation on your buttocks against whatever you are sitting on. You may realize that those sensations were there before I asked you to notice them. However, you probably did not experience these sensations before I asked you to pay attention to them. This body awareness, noticing how parts of your body feel at any particular time is instrumental to develop stronger communication muscles. If you are attempting to communicate with your spouse and are unaware of accumulating tension in your body, there is a good chance you will automatically react to remove that uncomfortable tension. You may do this by a fight or flight reaction such as yelling, withdrawing or acting out an addiction. If you choose to be aware of what is going on in your body, you can simply notice it and apply a creative maneuver to deal with the pain. Your conscious choices can include:

1. enduring the discomfort while you stay focused on your partner's discomfort
2. Sharing your feelings with your partner
3. Self soothing to relax and let go of tension

Many of us, especially men rarely put our attention on the sensations and feelings in our body. It is not difficult to do; simply take your attention off whatever you are focused on and consciously refocus onto your body. Pay particular attention to your heart and abdominal areas. There is a lot of information about us in our bodies that we can learn about but only if we pay attention to it.

I used to do day long stress management seminars and I would begin the seminar by asking the people in attendance about their stress levels. One particular seminar had a majority of men from a variety of racial and ethnic backgrounds. Many of them said that they had no stress. Then, a man from India probably in his 50's raised his hand and said:

"If you did this seminar 3 months ago, I would have said the same thing as these gentlemen- 'I have no stress.' About 10 weeks ago, I had a heart attack. I am recovering and I have been going to cardiac support groups and I am learning yoga and meditation. And let me tell you, I have stress in my life and body. I just wasn't aware of it. I have stress in my family life and at work. But now that I am aware of it, I can do something about it."

I thanked him and assured the audience that I did not pay him or arrange his statement in advance. I had their full attention for the rest of the day!

Another important aspect of body awareness and its relationship to effective communication is noticing if your energy is focused in your head and face or deeper in your body such as your abdominal area. This kind of awareness takes patience and skill. In order to understand this concept, you may need to do your best to catch yourself when you are starting to feel defensive and/or combative. Then notice where you feel the energy in your body. Often as a person gets defensive, his energy rises way up in his eyeballs and head. It is as if that part of the body becomes a shield to protect the more sensitive areas of the body such as the heart and belly from hurt and fear. What usually follows is over-reactive, quick and superficial responses that serve to protect oneself from the perceived attack from the spouse. As you become aware of the automatic rising of energy to the eyeballs and head, you can consciously refocus on your heart and belly areas where much of your more vulnerable emotional sensations are experienced. You can then remind yourself that your partner is not the enemy and you are not in danger. See if you can actually feel the energy in your body redistribute from your eyes, face and head to the center of your body where your vulnerable feelings are located.

Another way of using body awareness is to notice the quality of your voice. If you are panicky, defensive or reactive, your words seem to be high in your throat. Take a deep breath and calmly express yourself and you will discover that there is a different quality to your voice. Your voice is deeper and richer. If you notice, the sound that emanates as you yawn is deep because it is coming from deeper in your body. Practice catching yourself when your words are coming out higher in your throat. Notice the feelings in the center of your body that you were avoiding feeling by speaking high in your throat. This higher pitched, faster paced speech is an unconscious attempt to shield you from those feelings. Instead, breathe into the belly, exhale and speak from that calmer, centered place.

The Gravitational Pull of Inertia

When a couple seeks therapy there is usually a power struggle going on between them. Each partner typically thinks the following: "If you fix my partner then everything will be ok. I feel like a victim. Just change her/him and then everything will be ok." The feeling in the room is that there are two enemies fighting each other. What I impress upon couples in my office and upon couples reading this book is that you are not your partner's enemy—and your partner is not your enemy. We have all been handicapped by the limitations of our past in how to deal with pain constructively and in knowing how to be a healthier couple. We have all developed habits and patterns that do not work. We have allowed ourselves to exercise these habits and patterns until they have become familiar. Since we have acquired these habits and patterns, it is easy to fall into the habit of repeating the same thing we did the day before. When this happens, we stagnate as does our relationship. A lifeless or inert relationship is one where nothing new is happening; where there is nothing being positively created.

Learn to recognize the best in your partner. If your partner engages in some hurtful behavior or remark, remember that the motive of your partner is not to hurt you. And also, remember that your motive is not to hurt your partner. There may be some self-protective, fight or flight responses happening that are not helpful but neither are they of evil intent. Remember that you both have this familiar pattern of dealing with pain that does not get you anywhere. Metaphorically (or literally) hold hands together and unite as you declare that you are going to make the existing state of affairs your common enemy.

The wonderful thing about uniting like this is that it will help you when you are in the trenches of everyday decisions, challenges and conflicts with your partner. You may still repeat the same behaviors as before, and that's okay. No one changes long-held survival reactions easily or quickly. Patterns are hard to break. Instead of: "You see there is the same old thing; you never change," you focus on the positive changes that did take place between you. Build on the small positive gains that each of you accomplished. It is a good idea to let the small relapses of old behavior go and return to the more mature behaviors of communications you are striving to do. With time and practice, there is a "tipping point" where the mature, positive behaviors come more naturally and the immature, reactive habits have less of a hold. People change much quicker when they feel successful about the changes they already have made.

Paul and Ginger

Paul and Ginger came into my office and were arguing and blaming each other from the first moment they arrived, which is not at all uncommon. They were obviously conditioned to negative interactions. Ginger came from a family that allowed her to always be in control. She had to be the care taker. She was so busy taking care of everyone's needs that her needs and wants were neglected. Interestingly, her partner came from a family where he was the only child and everything revolved around him and his needs and wants.

Paul was use to living in his comfort zone and Ginger was use to living out of her comfort zone. As a couple, this was creating more and more problems for her. She was becoming increasingly frustrated about always being the one that had to make things better. He complained that she should be more easygoing. Paul wanted Ginger to kick back and relax more. With their cooperation I helped them both to see that they could play a part in breaking through their problems.

He had to learn to do whatever he could to help her feel differently than she did when she was a young girl living with her family. To help her, it might be something as simple as asking if there was anything he could do to help her around the house. At the same time she needed to learn that instead of being the martyr, she could ask him for what she wanted with the new expectation of Paul coming through for her. Ginger's automatic perceptions of her partner had to change as well.

We initiated a process whereby every time either of them would slip into their old behaviors one would say, "Let's have a do over." Then they would respond by doing what was unfamiliar and less comfortable but more constructive for them both. Paul needed to stretch beyond his comfort zone and Ginger needed to learn how to be more healthily selfish. They embraced the process as they made changes together. Paul became aware that he needed to get out of his comfort zone more; Ginger became conscious of the fact that she needed to be more skillful at receiving. They were able to help each other through their problems by giving and taking, listening to each other and then applying what they had learned. He needed to work on his interpersonal "weakest link" which was self-absorption and practice being more thoughtful. She had to work on her interpersonal "weakest link" which was her self-neglect and practice better self-care.

Exercises to Develop Emotional Muscle

1. Think of the last conversation you had with your spouse where you reacted because your emotional buttons got pushed. Think about what fear got triggered. Decide to contain your reaction; endure your temporary emotional pain and stay connected to your partner. Ask your partner to have that conversation over again. Tell her you want to do a better job of listening. Have that conversation with your intention to stay connected as opposed to the earlier unconscious intention of not listening.

2. Pick a topic that you avoid having with your spouse. Remember that no matter what you feel as you have this conversation, you can self-soothe and breathe through your feelings. Do not work too hard to convince your partner of something or to expect a particular outcome. Before you have this conversation, ask your partner if she is willing to have a conversation about this difficult topic. Have a signal in advance, such as the Time Out signal that could be used if things get heated. Typically, no matter how difficult the topic is, if you are loving and sensitive to your partner, things will usually turn out ok. After you begin the conversation, if it gets too heated, use your signal, give each other a couple of minutes to relax and calm down, and then resume your conversation. Another way to develop emotional muscle is to have this conversation about a difficult topic while holding your partner's hand. This is challenging because when feeling unpleasant emotions, we typically act in accordance to that feeling giving our feelings much power over our actions. Holding her hand signifies that I may feel negative feelings; however those feelings do not disrupt my underlying love for you. When both people feel heard, see if you can hug each other to further emphasize the point that your emotional connection is strong no matter what you feel.

3. Have an emotional game of catch with each other. In order to have this catch one person has to express (throw) a feeling. The partner needs to practice being in "receptive mode" to catch the feeling. When in receptive mode, you drop any agenda you have to accomplish something such as change your partner's mind, defend yourself, etc. It is the mode you are in when you are not trying to control or change anything. You are not resisting whatever it is that your partner is saying. You are there in the moment with your partner, taking in her information. If bodily tension arises, do your best to relax and stay with your partner's agenda for now. You can repeat her words, say "Uh-huh" or nod. The key here is to practice being genuinely interested in the emotional experience your partner is having right now. Practice putting all your thoughts, opinions, and reactions on the back burner. Be totally attentive to your partner. Listen and forget yourself during her turn. Once you know that she feels heard and received (you can always ask her if you are not sure), then it will be your turn. Your expressions should always be in the form of "I" statements. Remember, your goal is to expose and inform with love, not to convince, punish or berate. Take a chance being vulnerable with your partner. Should things start to go awry, stop, do a brief timeout, and resume.

5

Two Partners, Many Characters

We Are Made of Many Parts

Much of the information in this chapter I learned from two people who had a major impact on how I work with couples, Doug and Naomi Moseley. They were the first to help me with direct experience of the sub-personality theory in psychotherapy, a concept first introduced by Roberto Assagioli, the founder of Psychosynthesis. The sub-personality idea is that we are not just one personality. In fact we are many characters all operating inside of us at the same time. This and many of the concepts in this chapter are critical to developing what I call 'adult patterns in relationships'. Our ultimate goal is to behave as two adults in a relationship.

We are made up of many parts. There are the loving parts, the kind parts, the independent parts, the dependent parts, the angry parts, and the selfish parts. These are some of the many parts of who we are. Our soul is also made up of the many different aspects of who we are. These various parts are triggered at different times and in different contexts as well as by others' behavior. Maybe in one context it would be easy for us to be caring and loving but maybe in another context it is not as easy. We may become angry and/or defensive. This is standard human behavior. Different situations trigger different parts of who we are.

When you are working, you are coming from a place that is different than when you are at a picnic with friends. In intimate relationships, different sub-personalities in partners can emerge at different times in a variety of interesting ways. A couple's sex life could be greatly affected by sub-personality reactions. That is why it is important to talk about these sub-personalities.

One of the more useful ways of looking at the idea of sub-parts when I work with couples is defining the parent, child, and adult as individual parts. There is an emotional state to us that feels young like a child,; another that that feels authoritarian like a parent; and another part that feels equal to others like an adult. The child part is constantly seeking for power, approval or security. The parent part is constantly managing, nurturing, praising, organizing or judging. The adult part is capable of maintaining a sense of oneself even when another part is criticizing or demanding. The adult part does not put other adults either below or above. It maintains an adult stability.

Here is one of my favorite scenarios; the kind I hear frequently in my office. The husband tells his wife that he is coming home from work by 6 PM to have dinner with the family. He ends up going out for a drink with the guys, or just stays late at the office. But he does not call to let his wife know. His wife gets angry. Later, the man relates his story to me. "I knew I was in BIG TROUBLE."

When a person says words like "I was in big trouble", he is feeling like a little person who is going to be in trouble by a big person. He is now projecting his fear of the big Mama, who, in this case, is going to scold and punish him because he did something he knew he shouldn't have done. That may lead him to behaviors such as not calling, withdrawal or deflecting and starting a fight. This is how the child part of the personality can take over and keep the relationship in jeopardy.

Likewise it could be that if he did call her and say he was late, his wife could have come from her "parent part personality" and have judged him and been hostile. She could have talked to him as though he was a child. This will often evoke the child response from a man. This little scenario is typical of an emotional dance that happens often with couples and requires knowledge of the different parts of their personalities to hopefully become more aware.

Many couples fall into the parent/child behavior patterns. These patterns will be either from a mother – son, or from a father – daughter pattern. These patterns can shift but many times one partner will feel more of the time like the child and the other person will feel more of the time like the parent.

The partner in the child role experiences the spouse as either a benevolent good parent or the critical parent/restricting parent. These behaviors can sometimes shift from one parent mode to another.

The partner in the parent role often sees the spouse as the compliant child, the rebellious child, the needy child, the child that has to be managed or a combination of all the above. A common remark from partners in the parent role is that they feel like they "have an additional child to take care of" when they speak about their partner. The person in the child role will often say that their spouse is always nagging at them. When a person says that his partner is nagging, he is most definitely in a child mode and insinuating that his partner is in the parent mode. These are stuck patterns that will not allow relationships to become passionate and alive. As long as a couple remains in this parent/child fixed pattern they will not be able to make progress as a couple. This is a common way people deal with pain. With awareness, courage and commitment these patterns can be changed.

However, when not worked through, these patterns can escalate and become more entrenched into the couple's behavior. The more the wife acts like the mother, the more her partner will react like the son, and visa versa. The same goes for the father/daughter pattern. In other words the more the person in the parent role acts like the parent, the more that person is going to trigger the other person to act like the child, and visa versa.

Should you fall into this parent/child behavior pattern, ask yourself, "Do I feel like a parent trying to manage a child?" or, do I feel like a child being managed by a parent in my marriage?"

Adult to Adult Conversational Patterns

The key to overcoming the parent/child, child/parent behavior pattern is to develop adult-to--adult conversational as well as physical intimacy patterns. When the adult sub-personalities are in charge, both people are defining and expressing themselves to each other. Both people are being receptive to the other's feelings, needs and perspectives. As discussed earlier, when a couple is learning to play "catch" with each other, they are developing their listening muscle and also their adult personalities. Maintaining these adult patterns is a key to sustaining the long hot marriage.

Developing Feeling Awareness

Building on the section of last chapter on developing body awareness, it is essential to know what you are feeling so that the "adult" personality remains in charge. All feelings are experienced in the body. Most feelings seem to be experienced in the abdomen or heart area. Throughout my years doing therapy, clients repeatedly report that they feel feelings of hurt, sadness, guilt and shame in the heart area. It seems like these feelings have in common the theme of loss, whether it is loss of a person, loss of "face" or any other kind of loss. Clients report experiencing feelings of fear mainly in their abdominal area. These fear feelings could run the gamut from the milder feelings of concerned and worried to the extreme feeling of being terrified. Not all people report experiencing the feelings in the exact same parts of their body or in the exact same way. Also, depending on what you are feeling, you may experience sensations throughout your entire body. For example, if you are experiencing fear, you may notice that in addition to butterflies in the stomach, you may have a tightening of your leg muscles, jaw muscles, etc. Many of us, especially men, are not in the habit of paying attention to our feelings or defining what they are. Yet, it is crucial to develop this skill in order to have these adult to adult conversations with our partners. Similar to developing body awareness, feeling awareness allows you to not get your own feelings in the way of listening to your partner. Also, you can only communicate clearly and without blame if you are in touch with your own emotions. If you believe you are one of those people who do not have a high level of feeling awareness, you may want to do the following simple exercise:

Think of moments in your past when you lost someone or something important to you. Bring yourself back there in your imagination as clearly as possible. Tune in to your heart area and notice what feelings are there. Notice what the rest of your body is experiencing. If you have a hard time accessing feelings, you may be tightening up and resisting your feelings. This is a habit many people learn as a way to avoid experiencing unpleasant feelings. If this is the case, allow yourself to relax more and imagine the memory again. If you still do not access any feelings, you may want to come up with another memory that has more emotional charge.

Another Personal Example

The following is an example of shifting from a parent-to-child interaction to an adult-to-adult interaction. There was a time when my wife went back to work for about a year and a half as a teacher. I went from a full time to part time practice and was able to stay at home more and watch our only child at the time who was two. (We now have two daughters, Arielle, 15 and Danna, 12). I loved being at home. It was a wonderful time and I really bonded with our daughter. She was a delight to be with. One day my wife came home from work and asked me if I had done some task that she asked me to do. I had not done the task. My initial reaction was that I was "in trouble." I can remember the panic feeling I had in my belly. I had definitely retreated to my inner child. I said quickly, "I didn't do it because I took Arielle to the park and we got so involved with feeding the ducks and geese that I lost track of time. When I got back home I totally forgot about the task." My wife told me that she was upset with me and she felt that she couldn't count on me. My response to that was to angrily tell her to walk back out the door, open the garage door, come back in and then say "Hello" and ask me about my day before getting on my case. My tone was harsh and attacking. At that point she shook her head and started looking at the mail.

I asked myself how old I felt when I said that. My answer was 6 years old.

As stated before, old habit patterns emerged and I had to recognize that I felt very young-- like a bad boy. When parents express feelings, children do not go around saying that their parent is just experiencing negative feelings. Children do not think that way. They are in their own orbit; their own egocentric world. Even though I was an adult, I had reverted to and was coming from that child place inside of me. I was not thinking of her as an equal adult who was experiencing upsetting feelings. Nor was I aware of my own feelings so that I can handle them maturely. I saw her as an authority figure with the capacity to punish me. Of course, none of this scenario was planned; it was an unconscious, automatic reaction. On the other hand, dealing with this situation like an adult requires conscious awareness and behavior.

Back to my tale of woe: I took a deep breath and asked her if I could have another shot at that. It was sort of like saying could we have a "do over". I told her I wanted to make a confession about something. This got her attention and she looked up from the mail. I said, "You came in the house and were disappointed, understandably so. You asked me to do something and I didn't do it. I got lost in the fun at the park and can totally understand how you could be angry and frustrated with me. I apologize for that. I need to get better at writing things down." What happened was, it brought out her adult part as opposed to her parent part. She experienced my caring for her even though earlier in the day I had not done what she asked. She softened and was a delight to be around for the rest of the evening. It always pays to be an adult! It never pays to be the child or the parent. It also brought out the part in her to be forgiving for my mistake.

Example of a Mother/Son Communication Dynamic

Here is a conversation between my clients, Melissa and David.

Melissa: "You never listen."

David: "I listen!"

Melissa: "When do you listen? If your head is not in a magazine, your eyes are on the TV! Is that what you call listening?"

David: "Let's face it, no matter what I do; it will never be enough for you."

This is a relatively mild discussion that is not particularly volatile. However, it could escalate to a more volatile situation, depending on the personalities of each partner. What makes this a mother/son type of communication pattern? Melissa said, "You never listen." She is criticizing him, which puts her in a position of power over him. She does not share with him about how she is feeling.

David says, "I listen!" He is defensive and not thinking about what she is experiencing and what is behind her words.

Then Melissa asks, "When do you listen? If your head is not in a magazine, your eyes are on the TV! Is that what you call listening?" More blaming and accusations.

Then David says, "Let's face it, no matter what I do, it will never be enough for you." He feels he could never please his mate, who has now become his 'Mama'. He has reverted to the *"son position"* because he is experiencing himself as inadequate, resenting the power that she has over him or more accurately the power he has unconsciously given to her. He is not seeing her as an equal who happens to be feeling a lot of disappointment in him.

A conversation like this will inevitably lead to either (a) more escalated energy between them, or (b) each of them giving up. Feeling even more frustrated than before, there has been no resolution or feeling of being heard.

One of the things I find helpful is to have couples *'do over'* their unhealthy communications patterns right there in my office. We go back in time and set up the interpersonal scenario that was problematic. In this case, Melissa and David had several opportunities to replay the dialogue so that the parent/child dynamic can shift to an adult to adult dynamic. There were several starts and stops with one or the other getting defensive, blaming or not listening. I would halt the conversation and have them do it again. Here is the last conversation between Melissa and David.

Melissa: "I am feeling very frustrated because you do not seem to be listening to me."

David: "I am sorry, I heard your words, but it is true, that my mind was somewhere else."

Melissa: "To be honest with you, I feel frustrated a lot because you put your attention on the TV, the computer and everything else but me. It makes me feel lonely and like I don't matter to you.

David: "Yeah, I have to admit I don't usually do what I'm doing now. I don't think I ever really just look at you and put everything aside while you're speaking. I don't mean to hurt you and make you feel lonely but I guess I do. I am sorry. (He tears up)
(Melissa tears up as well and reaches for his hand)

Let us look at what the differences were between the first conversation and the last:

1. Melissa's goal of communication changed. The first time she had a goal, unconscious or not of criticizing, which could reduce her tension, temporarily. That was her payoff; she could reduce her tension, but at his expense. The second time, her goal was to *inform David of what she was experiencing emotionally.* She was more vulnerable treating him as an ally who can listen as opposed to an incorrigible child that she has to discipline.

2. Instead of getting defensive, David had to relax and soften enough to receive her feelings. He expressed his own feeling instead of getting defensive. Most men live in their heads much of the time. David had to let his energy sink deeper into his body, feeling his feelings, and not just reacting to avoid his uncomfortable feeling. This is key, *to feel one's feelings.* Melissa had to do this as well when she began dialog number two. In the long term, it never helps to avoid feelings, and we all do it in a myriad of ways, including yelling, withdrawing, blaming, addictive behavior, infidelity and many other ways we act out.

3. David also "owned his stuff"; he was honest that his mind was somewhere else. Courageously admitting one's areas of weakness leads to a continued de-escalation of misunderstanding and pain so that the connection between the couple is increased. In other words, it leads the partners to feel closer than they did before.

4. The upward growth continues as Melissa opens up a little more, expressing her frustration. David's understanding and non-defensive response to her honest expression creates a more trusting environment which in turn leads to Melissa continuing to express herself.

5. David once again responds by recognizing his inexperience in listening and has the insight that what he is doing in the office is very different than his typical behavior. He apologizes for the hurt he has caused her.

This couple has, of course, not solved all of their problems. However more importantly, they are becoming closer in their relationship. As they continue a new pattern of communicating with each other, they will feel increasingly closer. This is the result of developing adult to adult conversations. Each person dares to look at his or her contribution to the problem and together, they create a safe environment where they can be listened to and understood.

Rachel and Gary: Shifting A Mother/Son Pattern

Rachel is a 41 year old who has a 6 month old daughter. She was brought up by a mother who she describes as a worrier and she has some of those traits also. She believes in following rules and being disciplined. Her husband, Gary, has two children from another marriage and Rachel has become an important figure in their life as an involved and caring stepmother. She has pointed out areas of parenting that she believed were not being attended to by the biological parents (Gary and his ex-wife). Rachel gets frustrated by some of Gary's parenting and can be critical and easily lose her patience at times. Gary is an easygoing man who has tended to avoid conflict in the past and indulges the children when it may be better to be more firm and teach them how to tolerate frustration. Rachel's way of giving feedback often provokes him and he reacts defensively and accuses her of being too controlling and demeaning.

Read the following two expressions that Rachel could say to Gary after he has not enforced the consequence they discussed for his 10 year old son who did not turn in his homework.

1. "Will you ever act like a father to your son?"
2. "It is frustrating to see you not following through. Could you please keep to our agreement? That is the only way I see things improving in this family."

Rachel did say statement # 1 to Gary and you can imagine his response. She immediately had evoked shame; the shame that a little boy may feel when he as been scolded by his mother. Then he responded with anger and resentment. Ideally, Rachel would have said expression # 2 and Gary may have responded more maturely. In therapy, I challenged Gary to respond effectively even when Rachel was stuck in that "mother" role. I asked him to see beyond her provocative words and pattern and recognize that she was in pain. I asked her to say Expression # 1 again in the session. He responded, "I don't like the way you said that and it makes me want to say something mean back, but I know you are just frustrated with me and I blew it. Let's try to fix my mistake." That is difficult to do after being triggered by her words, but it is certainly possible and ultimately advantageous because it breaks the mother/son pattern of communication. He responded with some understanding and empathy, admitted his error and wanted to remedy the situation.

Rachel needed to learn how to express herself more as in Expression # 2. She needed to share her feelings as oppose to deride him. She needed to see herself as an equal who may be more aware of the need for limits but is not superior to him.

Example of a Father/Daughter Pattern.

Rick and Jeannie are clients of mine who have been married for almost 20 years. Rick is 14 years older than Jeannie. This is his second marriage where he brings several children from his first marriage. As a child Rick's mother was sickly and complained a lot, leaving his father to be more of a caretaker. Jeannie was a twin sister. Their father was a tough and macho kind of guy who got into a lot of trouble. He had brain damage from being clubbed in the head when Jeannie was 7 or 8 years old. She had to grow up quickly and be responsible, taking care of the family and never really became aware of her own needs and desires.

Rick was a successful attorney who also became a successful businessman. He was the kind of man who was determined to get what he wanted— and usually did. He wanted to have more sex with his wife but went after it as though she owed it to him, and that she should submit to his needs whenever he desired. Rick could be classified as an 'egocentric' man. Life was all about him, and meeting his needs. And since he was the bread winner in the family, he felt that she should go along with his program. Jeannie often slipped into the "daughter role" either being the good girl or the rebellious girl. Rebellious girls try to meet their needs in an egocentric way. The agenda is more about breaking free from the "father" control as opposed to truly meeting her needs. We are all aware of adolescent girls and boys who are rebellious and self-destructive. This same principal applies when adults are acting from their "inner rebellious child."

As time went on, Rick and Jeannie became more entrenched in this power struggle, where he was insisting on having sex. His wife, however, dug in her heels and refused to have sex with him. She pushed him away more and more, punishing him for his unfair demand by withholding sex. She looked at sex as a way to please him, like a daughter pleasing her dad. His insistence on having sex often did not turn her on. If sex was all about his needs and not about hers, what was in it for her? This dynamic would shift to a mother/son dynamic as well where she saw him as the needy child and she had to mother him. In either case, she did not experience her own sexuality.

In therapy, she first needed to be aware of her automatic feeling reaction when her husband asked for sex. She said that she felt angry, as if she had to please him which was then followed by resisting his wish as a way to not feel trapped by his desire. She then learned that the "daughter within" felt obliged to follow his desires as if they were rules to obey; if she said yes to his requests, she would be acting like the "good, compliant" daughter. If she said no, she would be acting like the rebellious adolescent. The next thing to understand was that it was her choice whether to please him or not. She needed to experience her own capacity to see him as an equal; not above her or below her; an equal whom she could please or not please. As a free adult, she did not have to please him. Just as important was that as a free adult, she <u>could</u> please him. The more she saw her decision as a true choice, the more the "father/daughter" feel of the relationship faded and the "adult/adult" feel of the relationship became more prominent.

One more important concept that contributed to this shift to adult/adult was discovering her own sexuality. She needed to be curious about what he could do to please her. She needed to begin a process of experimenting sensually and sexually with Rick to experience her own preferences that were different than her husband's.

Rick needed to learn how to let go of his need to control and have the marriage all on his terms. He needed to understand that if he truly wanted his wife to want him, he needed to make room for her as a sexual equal, whose needs, though different, were as important as his.

A Lioness or a Lamb?

An amusing, yet enlightening example of a couple with a father/daughter dynamic was Renaldo and Julia. Renaldo was a tall, large man in direct contrast to Julia who was petite and slender. At the first visit, Renaldo was extremely angry. His face was red like someone who was about to explode. He complained about his wife's sexual inhibitions and how lacking their sex life was. He claimed that she was not living up to her obligations as a wife, despite the fact that he worked hard and she was able to stay at home with the children and have the comforts of an upper middle class life. Julia remained very quiet until he was totally finished. He then looked at her annoyed and asked, "Are you going to just sit there?" She replied sheepishly, "I was waiting for you to finish."

Renaldo was clearly acting out the role of the critical authority figure and Julia was desperately trying to be the good girl. The good news was what a quick study Julia was. She quickly recognized her part in the father/daughter dynamic and began being more assertive in the bedroom, discovering her own needs and becoming less concerned with doing things "perfectly" in the bedroom. Renaldo was so thrilled about her newfound sexual energy. By the 5th visit, Julia was initiating sex as much as Renaldo. At the 6th visit, things continued to go well. Renaldo could not be more pleased with the rekindling of their sexual relationship and Julia was continuing to enjoy her new confidence as well as her new sexual experiences with her husband.

At the seventh visit, Renaldo's ruddy face had returned. He was clearly agitated. The first thing I said was that it is normal for relapses to happen and if that was the case, we could deal with it. He quickly replied, "No, there was no relapse. But does she have to challenge me all the time? She is becoming a real pain. She disagrees with me on just about everything." I responded back, "Oh, I see. You want a lioness in the bedroom but a lamb in the kitchen, dining room and den." He said, "That would be nice!" I told him that what he was asking for was impossible. The changes Julia had made in the bedroom were going to extend to other parts of the relationship. He either had to have a lioness "throughout the house" or a lamb "throughout the house." There was no in between and no other choice. He responded to my explanation with an apparent surrendering of his unreasonable attitude. He said, "Alright- I guess I'll take the lioness."

Like Rick, Renaldo had to appreciate that the price he has to pay for the benefits of enjoying an adult to adult relationship with his wife was to give up his egocentric need to have things all his way. With Renaldo accepting this small price, this couple was well on their way to a much more satisfying relationship.

6

Choosing Connection Over Control

I n Chapter 5, we discussed how to deal with pain. We learned that we can deal with pain either by creating more distance or by developing a closer connection with our partner. This Chapter will discuss developing the emotional muscle to connect and be partners even in your darkest moments.   Typically, when people are in emotional pain, they break contact with each other by either reacting or withdrawing (fight or flight).   Staying in rapport with each other especially when the other person is the stimulus for your pain is a challenging task.   When your mate is in pain, you want to be able to allow her to have her experience and do your best to understand what she is going through. As you understand the concepts and develop the skills discussed in this chapter, you will be in a much better position to create the kind of environment it takes to experience a long hot marriage.

As mentioned earlier, children are egocentric. They want control over their life all the time; and they want approval all of the time. Children develop power struggles with their parents because they keep pushing for what they want. When the parent says, "No," the child may not accept that "No" and continue to push for what he wants until he needs to accept that limit. Also, the child in all of us wants to be perfectly loved, so, on some level we are looking for that ideal parent that is going to love us perfectly In summary, the child wants the ideal parent who will always give the child control and approval.

Harville Hendrix in his book, "Getting the Love You Want," talks about helping a couple go from an unconscious marriage to a conscious marriage. He talks about the unconscious marriage being based on the 'imago', which he defines as "a composite picture of the people who influenced you most strongly at an early age." He says, "We enter the relationship with the unconscious assumption that our partner will become a surrogate parent and make up for all the deprivation of our childhood." He states that in the unconscious marriage people are trying to become whole through their partners. The conscious marriage is the goal which is what this entire book is about.

When we get married, we unconsciously wish for the ideal parent to be our spouse. The truth is that our parents were not ideal parents and how can we expect our spouses to assume that fantasy role?   We have to remember that our spouses are not our parents. They have needs, fears and desires of their own. Realistically we should remember that they will not always be thinking about us or physically be there for us. After about six months into a relationship ill feelings emerge and the illusion of the ideal parent collapses. We become disappointed and disillusioned with our partner. If it hasn't dawned upon you before, it's time to realize that we cannot always have our own way and we are probably not going to be perfectly loved. This is reality.

Letting Go Of the Idea of Being Perfectly Loved

There are basically two ways people try to get what they want from others. They will either try to accommodate and adjust to please or they will try to make others accommodate and adjust to them.   We lie somewhere on that continuum between being an extreme accommodator or an extreme comfort addict who needs others to contort for us. In most marriages, one partner takes more of the role of the accommodator/adjuster who is constantly trying to please the other. The way this person tries to get love and have some control is by trying to get his partner to be happy. "If my partner is happy, then I will be safe and loved" is the unconscious thinking of this partner.

In this hypothetical couple, the other person has learned that the way to feel loved and safe is by having her partner prove to her that she is loved. If he asks her to sacrifice or be uncomfortable, she sees this as unloving. She is also frustrated that she doesn't easily get her way.

On the way to developing our adult part, we have to let go of the fantasy that we are being perfectly loved. We also have to let go of the fantasy that we are always going to get our way. The accommodator/adjuster has to give up on the idea that he needs to please in order for him to receive love all the time. He needs to realize that his partner will never be the "ideal parent" to him or a parent to him at all, for that matter. He needs to stop trying to please so hard by constantly giving.

The partner who insists on being comfortable at all times demanding that her partner flex and adjust to her wants, needs to be aware that she is using him to deal with her own discomfort or negative emotions. She needs to let go of the idea that she can always have her way. She needs to find ways to manage her anxiety or disappointment. A male client once came to me stressed and burnt out because he had spent his entire marriage trying to give his wife all the material things she wanted. He could not say no to her. He described a time when his business was doing poorly, but his wife still said she was traveling to London to see a friend, a trip that would cost thousands of dollars. He did not protest but felt angry and more anxious than he already was. He needed to learn how to say no. As he learned and applied this concept, she had to change her thinking. For example, she needed to accept that it was not the end of the world if she did not see her friend at that time. She needed to adjust to the immediate economic situation and support her husband as he was going through this trying time.

She could feel the desire to have a temper tantrum and had to continually remind herself to be an adult and let go of the fantasy of her perfect world.

It is important to realize that most couples do not plan on slipping into these parent/child roles. They slip into these roles as an unconscious attempt to get what they want. The person in the parent role, for example, unconsciously believes that by being in a superior position relative to the spouse, she will get more of what she wants. The person in the child role has the unconscious belief that by coming from this child part, he will get more of what he wants. In reality, the person in the parent role does not enjoy the child part she evokes in her mate. This creates an internal conflict for her. The man in the child role does not enjoy the parent part he evokes in her. He is in internal conflict as well. A part of him is trying to get what he wants by being in the child role and yet he dislikes the mother role that he evokes. (Of course, when we are unconscious, we do not see ourselves evoking what we do not want in our mates; we just see our mates as being the problem). Once you become aware of how you are trying to get control or approval from your partner through these roles that you unconsciously slip into, you can choose to step out of those roles. Once you realize that you will never be perfectly loved, you can drop these roles more easily as you give up trying to control your partner.

Once a person understands and accepts this concept of not being perfectly loved or realizes he will not get his own way, there is an opportunity to deal with relationships as they are, and life as it is, as opposed to the way they would like it to be. In order to have a successful relationship, partners need to negotiate and strike some kind of balance between what each person wants and needs.

Couples need to develop an "and relationship" as opposed to an "or relationship". It cannot be my way or your way; it has to be my way and your way. It cannot be just my feelings or your feelings; it cannot be just my way of perceiving things or your way of perceiving things; it has to be my way of perceiving things blended in with your way of perceiving things. In other words, we have two sets of realities. We often have two sets of desires, preferences and needs. We have to learn how to creatively deal with two willful people who have minds of their own. When we give up the agenda of trying to control the other person we can now learn how to connect.

Connecting With Your Partner

What does connection mean? If an elementary school child chooses to make an electric circuit for his science project, he first learns how to connect the wires and then discovers that when he pushes down the lever, there is a connection—and the light bulb goes on! Voila! We need to connect with our partners in the same way. There has to be a flow; a flow of energy. In order to reach this flow of energy, we have to remain open with each other. Remember, this is easier said than done when there is emotional pain involved.

Typically when we have problems, this is the time when we break contact. We break our connection by venting/yelling, or withdrawing. Venting is a very solitary act. The purpose of venting is to get rid of bodily tension. Connecting involves a different purpose. When I connect, it means I see you as my ally as I express my problems to you. I am treating you as a person with your own set of feelings. There is someone really listening to me as opposed to just being a "sounding board." A board is two dimensional and inanimate. My partner is three dimensional and alive.

It is not just you doing a solo when you speak. I often see couples who claim to be "communicating" when they are not really communicating at all. They are talking at the other person and of course the other person "listens" by talking right back at the other person. That is not connecting. Connecting is when you talk as if that person is receiving you; and the person listening stays with that other person until he has finished. In other words they stay connected. There is a flow of energy between the two people.

If I am going to connect with you I have to make 'I' statements, and the listener needs to not be on the defensive. He needs to remain open even if his fears could be instructing him to shut down to protect himself. The most important thing is that the couple is maintaining a connection between each other. In connecting, the goal is not to win; it is not to convince the other person you are right or you are wrong, or my way is better than yours. The purpose of connecting is just that, to have a bridge between you so that you both <u>feel</u> a closeness together.

Benefits of Choosing Connection Over Control

From the child's point of view, control is all important. The child wants to have what the child wants. When you're in a relationship with an adult, neither partner wants to feel controlled. This is the way it usually goes: "Every time I do something to try to control you, change you, and convince you, you're going to try to control me back." This is just human nature. One of the laws of physics states that for every action there is an equal and opposite reaction. That basic law of physics also applies to relationships. Understand that every time you try to control or judge your partner, you are asking to be judged or controlled yourself.

Serenity's Prayer

God, grant me the serenity to accept the things I cannot change, the courage to change the things I can, and the wisdom to know the difference.
—used in AA and other 12 Step Programs

The Serenities Prayer is a great guiding light for couples wanting to strengthen their connection. Remember that you have no control over what your partner feels, wants, says or does. Why not instead choose to use the Serenities Prayer to accept the things that you cannot change about your partner? You would follow that up by focusing on how you can be interpersonally creative and connect with your partner. By so doing, you are paving the way for your partner to connect back with you. Again, every action has an equal and opposite reaction. There is a cosmic aspect to relationships. When you use the Serenities Prayer as your guiding light, your partner will also possibly accept you more as well. This often happens without us even being aware. Sometimes power struggles are not obvious. One person may seem to really be in control, but the opposite is actually happening. The partner who is being controlled or submissive often finds a way to control back. The person who is exerting the control will probably lose out one way or the other. When you connect with a person, which means that you are creating an energy flow between you both, your partner may perhaps soften and the chances of your partner wanting to meet your needs is more likely.

Connecting involves giving up trying to solve the problem for the moment. It involves giving up trying to make it better, rescuing her from her pain, wishing she felt differently or getting the outcome you want immediately. Being a partner in pain means just being there, surrendering into what your partner and you are experiencing without changing anything for the moment.

The word "emotion" comes from a Latin root meaning "to move through or out." Motivation and motion have the same root word. Emotions move through us when we allow it. If we resist these feelings, all that does is ensure that the feelings will hang around, and use up our precious energy. If we allow feelings to flow from our partner to us and from us to our partner, by "having an emotional catch" they come and go just like clouds in the sky. The analogy I like to use is that the sun is always shining even when it is cloudy outside. As soon as the clouds pass, the sun is visible again. Likewise, as you give and receive feelings and stay in rapport through pain, the love underneath can shine and warm each other up as the feelings pass through.

Staying in rapport with your partner always serves you; power struggles and control work against you. Connection has its initial pain because you have to mourn the idea of being perfectly loved. You have to accept the idea of not getting your way, which is a reality check. As you learn to connect emotionally, you are an adult treating your partner as an adult acknowledging his or her own different sets of feelings, needs and perceptions.

Exercises to Feel Closer to Your Mate

1. Sit across from each other and look at each other. Imagine loving energy coming into the crown of your head from the heavens. Breathe this loving energy into your heart area. As you exhale, imagine the loving energy coming from your heart and going directly into the heart of your partner. See the energy as a current. Feel the energy as warmth. At the same time, open your heart to your partner's loving energy entering your heart. Do this for several minutes as you maintain eye contact. Do this exercise whether you are in a good place with each other or not. If you find that you cannot do this exercise, first have an emotional catch with each other and then do the exercise.

2. Touch your partner in non-sexual places slowly and caringly, the slower the better. Concentrate on the feeling of your touch. Let your partner reciprocate after a period of time. Take in the feeling of your partner's touch on you.

3. Cuddle and do nothing else for a few moments.

4. If you are the kind of person that has difficulty with closeness, you can use words to hear yourself say things that you have never said before. For example, if you have a hard time saying, "I love you" say it to your partner. Repeat it, and each time say it with more feeling and more appreciation for him or her. You can take this verbal exercise as far as you want to. This is an exercise where the cornier the better. Let your positive feelings come out even if you feel awkward. "My heart goes a-flutter every time I look at you." Be authentic, but exaggerating somewhat is fine. The purpose here is to take the blanket off your own inner flame of feelings and passion.

.

7

Anger & Sexuality

Anger can be a destructive emotion. The raw, evolutionary purpose of anger is to destroy the other before he destroys you and to protect you from imminent loss. The problem is that as our brains developed, we became symbolic creatures. In other words, we could now get angry at someone or something that "symbolized" possible imminent loss. In modern days, it doesn't take a thief or bully to get us angry. We can become angry at other drivers "getting in our way" when we're stuck in a traffic jam. We get angry when our partner criticizes us. Since we, as advanced thinking beings, get angry toward people that are not really trying to destroy us, it behooves us to learn how to manage our anger in a way that will serve us without "destroying" someone.

We should not ignore our anger. Our anger is telling us that something is not right in our world. We need to learn how to contain our anger so we don't spill the contents of our emotion onto our partner. We need to "have an emotional catch" with our partner in our anger just like any other emotional state.

When a person or couple is angry, I often use a technique I learned from Doug and Naomi Mosley, mentioned earlier. I have the couple sit on the floor with pillows between them. Each partner knows they are going to be dealing with some feelings, and if anger comes up, they have these pillows to pound to get the energy going. The man looks at his mate and does not break eye contact. He takes in a deep breath and he lets out a growl from the depths of his belly exposing his anger to her. As she hears his growl, she remains calm and receives his growl. He is telling her, "This is what I am feeling right now. I have anger inside my body."

Why this exercise is effective, especially when one partner is feeling a lot of anger, is that words tend to dilute the raw experience of anger. When a couple does this exercise each person moves their anger from within to the other person. The person listening finds out that he was safe; nothing catastrophic happened to him. The couple connects in their anger as opposed to going on the defensive, resulting in both partners feeling closer to each other. When a couple communicates this way on a routine basis, they find out that anger is not such a threatening emotion. They realize that anger is just one more emotion that can be used to form a stronger connection between them both.

The key to doing this exercise is to make sure that your connection is stronger than the pain. The only way that you can ensure that the connection is stronger than the pain is to share as two adults whatever pain you have, allowing your partner to listen and hopefully become your ally.

Of course, it is not expected for every couple to sit there with a bunch of pillows every time they get angry, even though it is a useful technique. This can be done with words as well. The key is to develop the skill and the emotional muscle to contain your feelings so that you do not yell and scream. Remember that you can control your anger and you can express it constructively. You don't have to speak in a monotone; you aren't a robot; you do have emotion--and you are in control. Express yourself in such a way that you are not diminishing your partner. Your partner is your friend who has triggered some anger within you. Express your anger with respect to who your partner is as a human being. Say "I" statements. For example, "I am angry at you because you undermine me in front of the children."

Your partner can take your constructive criticism, and hopefully expresses him or herself as an adult as well.

What if you disagree? What if you totally don't agree and you believe that you did not undermine your partner in this example? That is not important at this point; emotional connection is the most important thing. You can discuss your point of view later on. You don't have to admit to something you do not believe in. You don't say, "You're right, I did undermine you." Nor do you have to defend yourself. You receive her anger and "catch the ball." Acknowledge and perhaps discuss how she is feeling.

The key is to establish an emotional connection, not to be factually correct. One of the worst things that couples do that destroy their connection is to go after and insist upon the truth. We must remember not to go after the truth prematurely; we need to first establish that important emotional connection. At this point, truth is irrelevant and will be resolved later. As a matter of fact, if your partner will ever see things more your way, it is only going to be after you establish a connection with your partner; and make the attempt to understand how she is feeling. Then there is a better chance that she will understand and perhaps see things from your point of view. Emotional connection first, the truth will work itself out later, if it's meant to be.

The Relationship Between Anger and Sexuality

The couple who learns how to face and navigate through their anger is inadvertently opening up their sexuality as well. You have seen movie scenes where a couple gets really angry and at the peak of their fury, one partner grabs the other and they kiss passionately. The scene then proceeds to where they are making passionate love to each other.

Anger is energy. Open up to it; you are stronger than any anger you or your partner feels. Connect through the anger with your partner. Keep eye contact, calm yourself and invite your partner to express more anger.

Anger does not destroy relationships; lack of closeness and understanding destroys relationships. I have seen many partners have affairs because of suppressed anger. Many of these couples that have been willing to work through the pain of an affair have learned to be more direct and expressive with anger between them. They begin to heal and feel a closeness and warmth they had not felt before. Some couples whose sex life had waned in the months or years before their affair were able to rekindle their passion in large part by being more open and constructive with the emotion of anger.

Another link between anger and sexuality that I have discovered is that the energy state of anger and sexual arousal are similar in that they are both intensely felt in the body. Similarly, it is helpful to learn how to manage feelings of arousal. A man who does not manage these feelings of arousal well may ejaculate too soon, or be too focused on his own release to be a sensitive lover. A woman may be overwhelmed by her arousal and suppress her sexuality. The man in this example is analogous to a person being reactive with his anger; the woman in this example is analogous to someone who is suppressing her anger. I have observed that partners, who learn to work with their anger, seem to be able to be more creative with their feelings of arousal as well. This leads to more of a give and take in the bedroom as the time of foreplay can be lengthened and the couple can experiment with new positions, ideas, etc. The point is that as you develop your ability to constructively deal with anger, you are:

1)   Opening up your sexual energies as well. There is a link between anger and sexuality.

2)   As you learn to contain the strong feelings of anger, you are using similar muscles to develop strong feelings of sexual pleasure to elongate and enrich lovemaking.

Human beings are not "selective stuffers." You cannot stuff or suppress your anger and think you will not stuff your passion and sexuality. If you stuff 90% of your anger, you will eventually stuff 90% of your sexual passion. The more you open to your anger, meaning, not to suppress the anger the higher chance you will have of a healthy sexuality. Reacting impulsively to your anger is analogous to lacking control of yourself to prevent premature ejaculation. A person who has premature ejaculation needs to learn how to practice self control before he gets to the point of ejaculation. Anger management is similar. Notice your anger and learn to manage it before you get to the point of no return and become destructive. Remember, for the average person, the purpose of anger is not to hurt or destroy. It is to connect- first with yourself to see what the anger is telling you and secondly to use this inner knowledge to teach your partner how to meet your needs.

SECTION 3

Sex & the Married Couple

8

Romance & Other Pleasant

Connections

In order to have a long, hot marriage, you first need

emotional warmth.

It is vital that we learn how to deal with our negative emotions because pain is what starts the disconnection between two people. We need to learn how to master communicating when we are expressing our unpleasant emotions in ways that make it easier for our partner to understand us. Likewise, we need to learn to listen so that our relationship becomes strengthened through our frustrations and discomfort we experience together. These crucial communication skills and the ability to develop emotional muscles pave the way for positive connections to emerge. Connecting through positive feelings and actions do not have to wait for our problems to go away first. Remember that we all have to deal with emotional pain for the rest of lives. However, learning to deal with pain effectively will make the positive connections more meaningful and fulfilling.

There are many ways to connect in positive ways with our partner. We need to visualize ourselves as having the power within us to make a difference in our partners' lives as well as in other peoples' lives in general. One of the biggest problem couples have in being able to connect successfully is passivity. Jack Barnard, my speaking coach and all around enthusiastic and caring person said, "At any moment, you can do one of three things- bring the energy down around you, keep it neutral or uplift it." Partners need to remind themselves continuously that in any moment they can do any one of those three things. A simple example from everyday life involves the situation of going to the check stand at your supermarket. Possibly, the checker has had a long day and is feeling tired. As a customer you can begin complaining about all the prices and how you should have gone to the other supermarket. The tired checker may now feel even more energy depleted after listening to you. Or, you can be all business and pay for your groceries and just leave. That would be a neutral encounter. Or, you can smile, say hello and even thank her for putting the eggs on the top rather than the bottom! There's an excellent chance that you uplifted her spirit is some small way. You left her happier than she was before she met you.

Romance is about doing or saying those thoughtful things that uplift the energy of your partner. There are a myriad of ways to connect romantically. You could connect with typical romantic gestures such as buying flowers for your partner. The partner thinks, "You thought enough about me to go and get flowers." It is the thought; it is the loving, positive energy behind getting the flowers. You could connect by complimenting your partner; or to acknowledge him for some effective parenting skills he has displayed or some other achievement--no matter how big or small. Let your mate know how much you love him with much feeling and sincerity.

The most important part of connecting emotionally to your partner is to STOP your busy life long enough to ask the questions 'what can I do?', or 'what can I say?', or 'how can I help my partner in some way?' It does not mean entirely changing your routine; it's merely interrupting your automatic routine. If you are like many people, your mind will often go to the question. "What's the next thing on my to-do list to get done?" I suggest that you consciously ask the question, "How can I put more energy towards my partner?" That is the most essential question you can ask. There are many ways to show your partner that you are thinking about her. Sometimes it is just stopping and looking at your partner, touching her softly, holding her, and expressing feelings of appreciation. The key is to create some time together every day or as consistently as possible to give loving energy to your partner. Write her a love note; it could be two or three sentences. Send her an email letting her know that you're thinking of her. Make a date with her.

I remember a couple where the wife complained that her husband did not give her enough attention, which is a familiar complaint. He expressed his frustration about her dissatisfaction, pointing out that he didn't drink too much, didn't cheat on his wife, did not abuse the kids, and earned good money. The husband was a CPA in his own private practice. I asked him to think back to his last client he had seen that day. It happened to be a couple who needed him to file their taxes. I asked him to recall the quality of his attention. What was he focused on? Was he even focused? He assured me that he was very focused on the couple as well as the documents they presented to him to file the taxes. I asked him to fast forward this image of being with the couple at work, to the image of coming home to his wife. I asked him about the quality of his attention on her; how did it compare to the laser-like focus he showed to the couple earlier at work. He laughed and got my message immediately. His attention was diffused. I asked him what would happen to his business if he gave the quality of attention to his clients that he gave to his wife. He answered, "I'd lose my business."

It is all a matter of attention. There is no part of our life that thrives without attention. If you do not water your plant, it dies. If you do not study, you fail the course. Why should relationships be any different? Focus on your partner every day for a certain period of time. Attend to her or him and let all other tasks, thoughts and concerns just recede to the back of your minds. Put your partner front and center! Do not starve your relationship. Just like food, we need to have emotional nourishment consistently.

One of the most important reasons for a relationship is the opportunity to develop our spiritual qualities, like kindness, generosity, forgiveness, and acceptance. These are also ways to connect emotionally to one's partner. Ask, "How can I be generous with my partner?" and that doesn't mean giving money, even though there is certainly nothing wrong with that. Ask yourself, "How can I generously give her of my time?" or "What is something I can do that I may not have done before that will make her feel loved and important?"

At times, in order to connect with your partner it may mean that you need to bring out something in you that is new or different. Maybe you are not the romantic kind of person, but one of the things that you can do is develop the courage to risk giving in ways that you may not have given before. This all adds to the sense of connection to your partner. You don't need to write a 3 page soliloquy. However, you can write a little love note and tell her how you appreciate all that she does for you—and that you love her deeply.

Trailblazing

We do not automatically connect with our partners because as a general rule, our parents and grandparents did not connect with each other emotionally. Life for them was about survival and making things better for the kids and not necessarily about spending time together and connecting.

There are people who may have had exceptional parents who were close, but most of us did not experience that closeness.

Connecting with your partner emotionally sometimes means thinking out of your own box. Read a book on romantic ideas or "Google" the phrase "romantic ideas." There may be ideas that require you to do something you have no experience doing or are not very good at. Give yourself permission to try something new despite that possibility. Take the time to stop and tell your partner what you are feeling, or perhaps connect through warm, gentle touching. This may be new to you or even make you feel a little discomfort or anxiety. But in order to connect with your partner you may have to tolerate some anxiety. By expressing negative feelings and being more vulnerable or expressing positive feelings, you are connecting with your partner, letting her know how much you care for her; and how you desire her sexually. I call this trailblazing because the old trails that were walked on before, by your ancestors as well as your current friends and family did not lead to the long, hot marriage. You need to be more attentive to the needs of your partner and yourself and blaze your own new trail that allows for increasing moments of warmth and positive regard for each other. Do not wait to "feel good" about your partner; create your own warm atmosphere and let your feelings flow from the positive connections you are trailblazing!

Scheduling Personal Thought Time

Time management experts say that scheduled activities always triumph over unscheduled activities and are always a higher priority. Schedule 2-5 minutes per day thinking about how you can be thoughtful, romantic and/or kind to your partner. Do this perhaps in the morning in the car on the way to work before you start your busy day. Establishing this routine each day will pay huge dividends in your relationship. Business experts and consultants say that you should not just jump into your day, but step back, plan, and make your priorities—and then jump in. They say this because they have found that the most successful business people plan this activity on a daily basis. Relationship success is no different. It requires vision, thought, and of course- follow through.

Scheduling Couple Time-Joel and Marisa

Setting priorities requires saying "No" to some things and saying "Yes" to others. It's called boundaries. The desire to have a good relationship will fall flat if you do not spend constructive time together. The biggest problem for many couples, especially those with children, is they literally run out of time to spend that special time together. I am working with a couple who has challenging time issues. Joel works long hours as a marketing VP for his company and gets home most days by 8 PM. Marisa gets up at 4 AM to begin her day by exercising. The rest of her day is filled with being a mother to two young children, volunteering in the classroom, preparing meals, etc. By the time Joel comes home from work, she is ready for bed. To remedy this situation, Joel is making the attempt at being more creative with his current work schedule. He plans to work later than usual two days a week so that he can be home for dinner on three evenings of the work week. With this arrangement, he can help with some of the chores with the children, and let his wife take a break. After that, they can spend quality together with both kids in bed.

Marisa also has to learn to say no to her kids and to some of her other activities. She is a dedicated mother and she spends much time driving children to dance classes and other activities. We brainstormed on what the children could possibly do without to give her very crowded schedule a little breathing room. I suggested that she find 30 minutes during the day, especially the ones when her husband was coming home earlier, to take a little nap to energize herself or simply do something enjoyable. This way, she would have more energy when she is having quality time with Joel.

Improving Quality of Couple Time-Katie and Lyle

Childless couples as well as couples who have children may have similar problems. Katie and Lyle were examples of a couple who had no children and still had no quality time together. Katie was a psychotherapist who worked late and was home by 8:30 PM during the work week. Lyle was a manager at a software company who worked from 8 AM to 5 PM. By the time she got home at 8:30 PM, he was tired and had no energy left for her. Katie wanted to eat a light dinner and hopefully get to spend some time with her husband each evening. She described herself to me as sexually frustrated.

Lyle described his day this way: "I get up in the morning like a rocket ship launching into space. I quickly eat a breakfast and get to work on time. I do what I have to do at work and am not very good at delegating so I end up doing other people's work as well. I do not take a break. I typically work through lunch and I leave work around 6 PM. I get home, eat dinner and by the time Katie gets home, I am spent."

He learned the importance of planning his day and making choices that would let him have some energy for his wife. Just like budgeting your money, you cannot spend all your energy in one place. Lyle was spending all his energy at work. We worked together on his making more positive decisions in better self care, developing relaxation skills and learning to delegate. After a few weeks, his days looked something like this:

He would get up at 7 AM and do 5-10 minutes of meditation. He would get ready for work and eat a decent breakfast. At work he would stop every hour for one minute and

1) Do a breath check to see if he was breathing deep into his abdomen for relaxation. Relaxation conserves energy whereas stress reduces energy.

2) Determine if any of his recent or future tasks could be delegated, and to whom.

3)   He took one 5-10 minute break in the AM where he went outside or just sat quietly at his desk. At lunchtime, he took 30 minutes for lunch, with no work. He took another 5 minute break in the afternoon and left no later than 5:30 PM unless there was an emergency which rarely happened.

4)   When he got home after work, he had a snack and then took a half hour nap. By the time his wife got home, he either had dinner on the table or they went out to eat. Their lovemaking increased significantly. Katie was much happier and Lyle had more self esteem, increased health, and much less stress.

There is often resistance to spending time together because of outside interruptions, such as work. When you take an honest look at what your circumstances are and are willing to make positive changes such as Lyle did, then you may have time and energy to spend with your partner.

Exercises to Increase Romance

Each week, do one romantic gesture towards your partner. Examples include:

1. Write a love poem.

2. Write a love note and hide it in a place he will see later on.

3. Ask your partner to dance with you in your living room.

4. Sing a love song to your partner.

5. Before your spouse comes home, light candles everywhere and meet him naked when he comes to the door.

6. Before he comes home, put rose petals everywhere and have a romantic dinner waiting.

7. Ask your partner what would be a romantic thing he would like, and do it.

8. Plan a date that consists of some quiet time together such as a gondola ride, a walk on the beach, horseback ride, bicycle, ride in the country, etc.

9. Be willing to go outside your comfort zone. Go beyond what you usually do to fulfill your partner's romantic fantasy—whatever it is.

9

The Making of a Great Sexual Partner

W hat makes a great sexual partner?   The short answer is- a partner who engages in loving and pleasurable foreplay with his mate. The American Heritage Dictionary defines foreplay as "sexual stimulation preceding intercourse." I am expanding the definition of foreplay as anything you do or say with your partner that creates warm or hot feelings. By that definition, the whole book has been about foreplay. Perceiving your partner in the best possible light allows for warm feelings to develop. High impact partnering can lead to raising the emotional temperature between the couple.   Dealing with pain constructively removes the blocks to sexual desire and creates a closeness that can lead to more lovemaking. We discussed the relationship between anger and sexuality and how the couple who can stay in rapport through anger will increase their capacity to elongate and enrich lovemaking. Doing romantic gestures and creating a lifestyle that makes time for couple togetherness creates warm, pleasant feelings between partners and sets up the conditions for enjoyable sex.

However, let's go back to the dictionary definition of foreplay. Foreplay is somewhat of a misnomer since it implies that sexual intercourse is the main event. Foreplay becomes a means to an end. A great lover treats foreplay like the main event. That does not mean that you never have intercourse. Nor does it mean that you do not plan for intercourse by having birth control or holding back ejaculations until inserting your penis into your partner's vagina. It means that you savor the process of sensual and sexual touch from the very first touch. This chapter discusses both the necessary mindsets as well as the behaviors of the great lover. You will notice that being a great lover has less to do with what you do than how you do it. It has more to do with creating mutual pleasurable physical exchanges than creating a virtuoso performance. In order to do be a great sexual partner, you need to:

1. Choose connection over performance
2. Be in the present moment
3. Create Intensity by breaking free from "your image."
4. Be a loving lover
5. Be playful.

As you read, notice how linked these five facets of sexual experiencing are.

Choosing Connection over Performance

I have learned that the key to a good speech is not a perfectly sounding, smooth series of words. Speaking is not a performance. Having good eye contact, focusing on how I can help the people in the audience and genuinely accepting them is far more important than anything else in determining how effective I am as a speaker. In other words, connecting with my audience is paramount to having a successful speaking career.

Fulfilling sex also depends on this emotional joining between partners. The problem is that the way we learned about being great lovers had absolutely nothing to do with being connected partners. For men, being a great lover had more to do with performance. It had to do with having hard, erect penises that could last and last and last. It had to with women getting many orgasms. This is not representative of what makes a good lover; as a matter of fact, our attempts to perform well, and be great lovers, are the very things that have made us poor lovers. We have to actually unlearn a lot of the information we have learned as teenagers, since much of that juvenile information is still guiding how we think and act in the bedroom as adults. When focused on performance, you are self-involved, hoping to impress or meet a certain calibrated measure of what it means to you to be successful. In performance mode, you are trying to force things to go a certain way. When this happens, you are not focused on your partner; there is no bonding or true merging happening. It is better to be naked; not necessarily physically but more as in the sense of letting her see you as you are-flaws, imperfections and awkward sexual moments. Rather than expect to always have a seamless performance, instead be willing to adjust what you do, your position, etc. to increase the pleasure of your partner or yourself and enjoy the process. This allows you to focus on her and a feeling of intimate closeness can be experienced.

Be in the Present Moment

Many of us are rarely in the present moment. We get caught up in thoughts about the past and the future. This obstructs us from fully experiencing what is going on now in this very moment. We all have experienced what it is like to be absorbed in the moment. If you have been out with nature and fully appreciated a running creek or beautiful sunset, you have had this experience. Being totally immersed in the enjoyment of your favorite food or skiing down a mountain, you are totally in the "now." In moments like these, you are not thinking; you are experiencing. In the midst of having an orgasm, you are in the present. You are not thinking about what happened earlier in the day or what might happen next or in the future. These described experiences often give us glimpses into what it feels like to be totally in the present.

When with your long term partner, it may not be automatic to be in the present moment when doing foreplay with your partner. You need to be aware of where your mind is; are you caught up in thoughts or are you focused on your partner as well as your own enjoyment of your partner? If you are not in the present moment, notice what you are thinking about. If it is something that needs to be discussed, then place a pause on the lovemaking, talk it out and see if you can return to the lovemaking with a more present and attentive approach. When present, you are more focused on the sensations of sight, hearing, touch, taste and smell. Notice your partner and take in the sight of her. Notice the sounds of lovemaking. Notice the physical sensations where you are touching with your hands and other parts of your bodies. Also, notice the emotional feelings of closeness and savor the experience. Taste your partner; her skin, her mouth, her genital area. Enjoy the aroma of your partner's body or breath. Of course if any of these sensations are unpleasant and something can be done about it, ask your partner to take care of it. (For example- brushing teeth or taking a shower) You can return to whatever you were preoccupied with mentally after you are done making love to your partner. Lovemaking is an opportunity to enjoy your own ability and right to experience the present moment fully.

Create Intensity by Breaking Free From "Your Image"

Many couples complain that something is missing in their lovemaking and I have discovered that the missing link often is "intensity." The major block to intensity is self-protection. What people are protecting is their "image."

Think of one's image as an outer covering. One's "image" is not who one is. If I am wearing a long, black coat, would I then be a long, black coat? Of course not! First, there are clothes you can not see underneath.

Underneath my clothes is my body. Of course my body contains my feelings, thoughts, fears, cravings, fantasies, etc. People's created images that they hold on to are similar to the long, black coat. We spend much of our time creating the image we think will help us get to where we need to go. Life becomes less spontaneous and words and actions are calculated and more controlled to keep this image going. However, letting go is what works best in the bedroom. Dare to express yourself more intensely. Risk looking foolish or exposed as you profess your love to your partner. Let your love or playfulness come out through your touch. The less you are concerned about how you present yourself, the less you will hold back your passion.

A wife was complaining about her husband's monotone way of saying that she looked pretty. She said it sounded as if he knew he had better say something because she was all dressed up to go out, but that he probably was not <u>affected</u> by how she looked. I asked him if that was true and he said, "No, I actually was aroused but we had to go out; other wise I would have wanted to make love to her." She said, "I never would have known that you felt that by your tone of voice." This man had learned to keep his feelings under control. Even though there are times it is best to keep feelings under control, this was not one of those times. In the session, he practiced speaking in a way that matched his intensity. Eventually, he allowed her so see how affected he was by her. He looked right at her and said, "Yeah- when you were dressed like that, I wanted you badly." His tone was full of excitement and his eyes lit up as he was speaking. He had created intensity between them just by allowing his emotions and passion to be more visible to her.

The intensity this husband demonstrated was foreplay at the very best. Breaking through his image of the controlled, logical male through words, tones, posture, smiles and eye contact was far more of a powerful aphrodisiac to his wife than any particular technique or position.

Being a Loving Lover; the Case of Nate and Corinne

The following is an example of a client couple, Nate and Corinne, where sex was a power struggle and how they were able to successfully shift the struggle into an adult-to-adult sexual relationship. Nate's mother died when he was one year old. His older sister tragically died when he was nine years old and she was eighteen. Nate had two daughters from his first marriage. When his first wife divorced him, his wife had played the victim role during their marriage. The two daughters had chosen to "mother" their mother and had chosen to keep their father out of their life totally. Obviously this was a man who came into his second marriage to Corinne with a history of loss of significant females. Corinne came from a family where achievement was emphasized and emotions were de-emphasized. She had learned to be independent and had become a successful CPA with her own private practice. Her father had cheated on her mother often, and she had come into the relationship with some distrust of men. She married Nate at the age of 41, and this was her first marriage.

They came in with the complaint that he was frustrated because she didn't want to have sex with him. She was frustrated that he didn't have "slow hands"; he did not touch her slowly, softly and lovingly. I asked Nate to come in alone. I hypothesized that since Nate had had so such maternal loss, that in the bedroom, he probably came from the abandoned child part of himself. I wondered if his need for merging with a female was so strong and his need for her touch was so overpowering that it was overwhelming for Corinne. Maybe his touch was too 'clingy' and the way he looked at her was too 'needy'. Corinne, being so independent could be turned off by his excessive neediness and she would shut down sexually.

To remedy this shut down I asked Nate what his typical reaction was when he first saw Corinne. He said, "Well, she's really a beautiful woman, and I get all horny." I replied, "That is a normal, healthy understandable reaction. However, before you approach her the next time for sex, I'm going to ask you to try a little imagery exercise. I know this is a little different, but I want you to try it. You have nothing to lose." After he agreed, I said, "I want you to imagine that there's this loving energy out in the heavens, and you're going to breathe it in from the crown of your head. You're going to feel that energy come in to your heart, and as you exhale, this loving energy is going to go out through your arms, into your hands, and out from your hands, into the universe. You're going to glance at your wife and see her as a person who needs to feel loved. Immerse yourself in this imagery and experience yourself as a conduit of this loving energy, and as you touch her, keep in mind, that you are this conduit of energy. That was the way the session ended.

The following day, I get a voice mail message from Corinne. In a happy and grateful tone, she said "Todd, keep talking to my husband, I'll see you next week."

An important aspect of becoming a great sexual partner is to discover that place deep inside of you that is love. Nate was able to change where he was coming from in his approach to Corinne. Instead of horniness and lust, he approached her with love. Do not wait for your partner to make you feel good. Find the place inside of you that is capable of caring for your partner. It is that part of you that gives for giving sake. Nate was going after Corinne from a sense of "lack;" a need to have her make up for his feelings of loss; he was looking towards her to soothe him. Using the imagery, he accessed a part of him that did not have a sense of lack. From that place, in that moment, he did not need Corinne to complete him; he was able to give from that place of love. I would define this place of love as that part of you that is part of the ever present capacity within you to focus on the wellbeing of the "other" without needing anything from that person in return in that moment. I am not saying that you do not need your partner as well; as a matter of fact, the more you come from this loving place, the more you will receive from your partner. It is the difference between two adults giving freely to each other as opposed to two needy "children" in a power struggle trying to get what they want from the other. Nate and Corinne had been acting out old family dramas in the bedroom. The dominant feelings here were anxiety, frustration and the occasional relief when one got his or her way. In contrast, you could say that when coming from the loving place that was described, giving and receiving is at a higher energy level where feelings such as warmth, compassion and joy are dominant in the experience. Even as you experiment and become more playful as described in the next session, remember to keep love at the center as you experience the many parts of each other in the bedroom.

Being Playful

For some people, it is easy and natural to be playful sexually. For many others, it is not. This section should help those that need to develop the playful side of their nature especially in the bedroom. The more you choose connection over performance, practice being in the present moment, break free from your image and come from love, the easier it is to enjoy playfulness with your partner in the bedroom. As you do practice the other four skills, you become less and less self conscious. It frees you up to be spontaneous and experimental. Start by practicing being playful outside of the sexual arena. Here are some suggestions:

1. Skip. Skipping brings out the childlike, playful side of you like almost nothing else. (Childlike is different than childish; being childlike can add a dimension to your life and relationship as long as the timing and context is right. Childish is more what I mean when discussing the parent/child patterns in couples). As you skip, lift yourself as high as possible and swing your arms. Get into it and go beyond your comfort zone. When you begin to feel foolish, exaggerate the movements a little more.

2. Sing a happy song no matter how well or badly you sing. When you are ready to stretch some more- sing to your partner.

3. Put on some rock and roll and dance. When you are ready, dance in front of and with your partner.

4. When by yourself, try fake laughing; let the laughter come from your belly. Open your mouth widely and let the sound of laughter come out loudly.
5. Challenge your partner to a friendly wrestling match.
6. Get into a tickle fight with her.

The above exercises will help you move past your self limiting comfort zones and help you have a greater freedom in being playful.

The following exercises will help you become more playful sexually:
1. Part of foreplay can be tickling and wrestling as discussed before.
2. Feed each other with a lot of sucking and licking. Use your body as a plate.
3. Ask your partner what her favorite sexual fantasy is and be willing to share yours.
4. If possible, act out the sexual fantasies you are learning about from your partner.
5. Dance erotically with your partner. Have fun with it. Gyrate your hips and dance closely and sexily with each other.
6. Women can take a visit to Victoria's Secret and pick up some lingerie to wear as part of sexual play. If the woman has some fantasy that involves the man dressing up, he can dress up as well.
7. Teasing and seducing can create a healthy tension and increase arousal. The intention has to be playful and not mean spirited. The goal is not to frustrate your partner; rather it is to tolerate the tension of the excitement until you give in to the pleasure and sexual impulses. Sexy dancing, strip-tease, and refusing to comply with sexual requests are all ways to playfully arouse and titillate. Also, the way you touch your partner and where on his body can create a playful excitement.

8. Alternate between being the seducer and the seduced. It is usually more enjoyable when both partners can act out both parts at different times.

Power Struggles in the Bedroom

In Chapter 6, we discussed choosing connection over control and about power struggles that can happen in a relationship. Power struggles can continue into the bedroom.

As marriages continue, the sexual arena can become a place where each person is vying for control. One person maybe wants sex more than the other. Possibly, one person wants to do one particular sexual act and the other person does not. Power struggles in the bedroom cannot be separated from the power struggles out of the bedroom. Sexuality is energy, and so are the frustrations, desires, and longings that we have outside of the bedroom. As each partner learns to deal with conflict in an adult way out of the bedroom, they can also learn to extrapolate that understanding into the bedroom as well.

As an example, one kind of power struggle is when one partner has a different pace than the other. The expression I often hear is that women are like crock pots, men are like microwaves. He may want to have sexual intercourse or oral sex and maybe she isn't ready just yet. She may require more romance outside the bedroom and more foreplay once they are in bed. He may want the sexual act that leads to orgasm quickly and she may want more time to warm up.

What happens then is that each partner will dig in and hold on to their positions and nothing is resolved. It is difficult for the power struggle to end, because as long as each person is in their childish behavior pattern they are each fighting to get what they want. The man in this instance who is fighting to have more ejaculations becomes resentful because his partner is being obstinate and exercising her right to say "no." He says, "I mean it's just sex for crying out loud, why can't we just have it?" On the other hand, the woman says "I'm not going to give you sex, because it feels like it's all about you and not about me."

The first step in shifting out of the sexual power struggle is to be willing to tolerate the tension of being different than your mate and not make each other "wrong" for having different sexual preferences or priorities. If he wants sex more than you do, accept that he wants sex more than you do. That is very different than feeling *obligated* to meet his needs. If you feel obligated, you will do one of two things. You will either comply and have half-hearted sex or you will rebel and withhold. This relates to the second step of shifting out of the power struggle which is – Be true to yourself. Acknowledge your own particular preferences and desires. You are not wrong to feel differently than your partner or have less or more sexual desire at any particular time. The third step is to accept that you will not always get what you want sexually from your mate.

From this place of acceptance of difference as well as being non-judgmental of your partner or yourself, you can better tolerate the tension of inevitable conflict; inevitable because since you are two different people, there will probably be many times that you are not perfectly in synch with your partner. Paradoxically, as you accept the tension of conflict, you are now in a position to choose whether to stay firm or to yield to your partner's request. Either way, it is a choice and there is no obligation to please him or not please him in any particular instant. You can yield to his requests and still be true to yourself since you are choosing to be generous. If you decide to stay firm with your position, you are not doing it to control him or regain a sense of power, since you already have your own sense of power. The only reason to not yield is if you decide that it is not in your best interest to flex at this particular time.

There are times to have a quickie with your partner if that is what he wants. There are times to insist on more foreplay as well as more emotional sharing and romance. Do your best to live on both sides of the fence. Sometimes do it your way and sometimes do it his way. Take turns just like any game you would play. Remember- the key is to be aware of any sense of obligation or "have-to" and once aware of it, realize that you are an adult and have the power to say both yes or no.

The Inner Critic in the Bedroom

It is important to become aware of your own internal critic. If your partner is being critical of you it does not necessarily mean that you also need to be critical of you. You need to be more aware of, and have more confidence in yourself and your abilities, and to be ok with you, even when others are not. That does not mean that you do not learn from what others say or that you do not make changes. It does not mean that if your partner asks you to stop doing something that does not make her feel good that you keep doing it. You want to be sensitive to your partner and receptive to the feedback she is giving you. There is a difference between being receptive to feedback and psychologically beating yourself up by telling yourself you are bad or not good enough. If you expect to always please your partner, you are setting yourself up for disappointment. Pilots spend much if not all of their airplane trip getting back on course. They are rarely on course for long. It requires constant adjusting and correcting. Think of your sexual relationship in the same way. If your partner is expressing some displeasure, it only means some adjustments need to be made. Don't waste a lot of time trying to be good enough in the bedroom. Instead, enjoy learning to dance sexually with each other.

Diving in Head First

As a child, I wanted to dive in head first off the diving board even though I had never done it before. I would get on the diving board with my intention to dive into the pool head first and at the last minute, I would jump in with my feet. I would get annoyed with myself and I would get back up on the diving board and I would get on the edge and I would jump feet first again. This went on for quite a number of times; each time I was determined to dive in, but when I got to the edge of the board I was afraid, so I would jump in with my feet. I found that the tenth time was not any easier than the first. I remember the moment when I was willing to go for it. I think the disappointment with myself overtook my fear of something bad happening, so I dove in head first—and nothing bad happened! Of course after that, it was easy to do it again.

In order to be a unique sexual partner, there are going to be moments where you are willing to open up to something new and unknown. Sharing something revealing about your sexual desires with your partner, perhaps bringing out your wild side in bed can feel risky. There is that uninhibited moment where you welcome the unknown and go ahead and experience that new part of yourself, just like I did when I dove in head first.

The inner child is looking for a way to go through life and marriage without any anxiety. The adult inside knows that there is no such thing. We have to pick the more useful anxiety over the useless anxiety. The useless anxiety is what happens when we avoid connection and intimacy. This is the anxiety of feeling disconnected and unsatisfied. Useful anxiety is when we have those moments where we take a chance; and dare to do something different. In these daring moments, we are most alive with ourselves and our partner.

The Case of Roger and Sarah- Deepening their Interaction in the Bedroom

Roger and Sarah was a couple that had played it safe for most of their 30 years. They had 4 children. The joke between them was that they had probably only had sex about 4 times. They both had their individual blocks. Sarah had some bad habits, like the fact that she would sneak candy bars, instead of telling her husband about it. She would hide the candy and he would find the wrappers. He was not that upset by her eating candy bars; it was definitely a case of her acting out like the little girl that did not want daddy to be upset with her. Sarah had been molested by a baby sitter when she was younger and tended to avoid sex. She viewed sex as a very scary thing. She was able to see that it was the "wounded child" part of her that viewed sex as scary because as a girl she had no control and sex evoked this sense of powerlessness. She started to identify more with her "adult" part that had control and could choose how she used her body sexually. We worked on those issues to the point where she felt better about herself sexually and wanted to have a better sex life with Roger. Much of the therapy was also about alleviating guilt and shame that resulted from the fact that- despite being violated, there was a part of her that enjoyed the stimulation and attention. (This is a common source of guilt for victims of childhood molest). As her shame lessened, so did her habits of sneaking food.

Roger had his own resistance to having sex also. Even though he seemed to want sex, I sensed he was really ok having a sexless marriage at the same time. He did not seem too upset about the lack of sex and would deflect the topic of sex as quickly as his wife during our sessions.

I gave them the assignment of just touching each other, using a soft touch in non-genital areas. They were to do this for about 10 minutes every day. The reason I gave this assignment was that when people lose their sexual passion or resist the sexual act for one reason or another, they often will stop being affectionate or touching altogether. This assignment was a way to reintroduce themselves to each other.

Later, I get a phone call from Sarah telling me that she couldn't do this assignment anymore, because when she touched Roger, he said, "Oh my God! When you touch me it makes my skin crawl." Of course that was hard for Sarah to hear. She felt rejected and it brought out her feelings of inadequacy as well as shame. I told her, "I understand how hard that was for you and I can understand why you would not want to go through that again. But remember Sarah, this was not about you, even though it seemed that way."

For 30 years they had pulled away from each other at the first sign of rejection. One of the affirmations I had Sarah repeat to herself was, "I am ok and my self esteem does not rely on Roger accepting me." It was important that she talked to herself like this before she touched him again the next night. I let her know that I understood there was a big part of her that did not want to do this. I said, "As you touch him if he comes up with the same feeling that his skin is crawling, take a couple of deep breaths, and then say to yourself, 'I'm ok, this is not about me.'" What she needed to be was the adult and to stay connected with him physically and emotionally and say: "Tell me what's going on with you. What do you mean when you say your skin is crawling?" She said with some reluctance, "OK, I'll try that."

When they came in for their session the following week, they looked happy. They each took turns telling me exactly what had happened the night following the conversation I had with Sarah on the phone. Sarah followed my directions and did touch Roger. He said once again that he felt like his skin was crawling. Sarah asked him what was going on. At first, he said absolutely nothing, and then he said that he did not know. Sarah asked if she could touch him again to see how his skin feels. At this point, Roger said, "Well actually now that you say that, I just know that it feels like when my mother used to touch me; it wasn't like she was molesting me in any way, but her touch was so needy. I felt like I disappeared when she touched me. It was all about her needs." Then Sarah surprised him when she said, "Ok, tell me more." At that point Roger broke down into tears. They held each other a few moments and then Sarah said, "I would like to do this again." She added, "Remember I'm your wife, I'm not your mother." And he said, "Well that's fine." They proceeded to go beyond what I asked them to do for the assignment and they ended up having intercourse 3 times that week, which is about 3 times more than they had in years.

This is a wonderful example of a couple doing avoidance that we all tend to do when uncomfortable feelings come up. And the truth is that at times, sexual intimacy and getting closer to your mate could bring up uncomfortable feelings for one reason or another. In Sarah's case, she was protecting herself from feeling inadequate, dirty or ashamed and Roger was unconsciously protecting himself from feeling like he would dissolve and disappear into the absolute neediness of a female. Being willing to go deeper by experimenting and then not reacting or avoiding their problems gave them the opportunity to have a stronger connection and ultimately they experienced the emotional breakthroughs that it took for them to have a healthy sex life.

Creative Monogamy

Let's be honest. It is natural in a long term monogamous marriage to sometimes fantasize about being out of the relationship and/or to be attracted to another person. We are complex human beings with many parts as has been discussed in this book. In most cases, the ideal is to be free to reveal all that you are experiencing and feeling with your partner. Sharing conflicted feelings or about attractions towards other people can actually bring an intimate couple closer. It requires a more mature, less egocentric attitude. There is a big difference between actions and sharing feelings. If one shares with his mate that he is sexually attracted to another that is very different than acting it out.

Ambivalence

In Robert Beavers book, "Successful Marriage," in the chapter titled Attributes of the Healthy Couple, he states, "I have rarely seen any respect for ambivalence in dysfunctional couples." When it comes to any sort of commitment, there are often ambivalent feelings. The definition of ambivalence is ambi-meaning two and valence- meaning charge. An example of ambivalence is- you can want to be married and you can also want the freedom of being single at the same time.

An acquaintance told me how he had gotten married and on the last day of his honeymoon, he woke up and looked at his sleeping newlywed wife and said to himself, "Oh no--I married the wrong woman." After a week at home his wife asked him what was bothering him. He replied, "Nothing." She said, "No, something is wrong, you have been nitpicky and critical of me ever since the last day of our honeymoon." He said quickly, "I am sorry; I'll try to be nicer." She responded. "Think about it, something has been going on with you ever since the last day of our honeymoon." He remembered the thought he had been suppressing since the honeymoon had ended. He tried to dismiss it and promised he would be nicer, but she was relentless. She continued asking him what was going on. Finally he said, "Well, I looked at you and I got scared thinking that I had married the wrong woman." She replied, "Oh is that all; you'll think that hundreds of times!"

This was truly a wonderful response that reflects real life with all its complexities and mysteries. Most of us are still trying to live up to the fairy tale of being Prince Charming and Sleeping Beauty living happily ever after. It is a nice and simple thought but we are not that simple and far more interesting! The last time I checked with this acquaintance, he and his partner seemed to be developing a strong, happy marriage.

Attraction to Other People of the Opposite Sex

In Bernie Zilbergeld's book, "The New Male Sexuality" in the chapter "Am I Normal or What?" he says: " Since it's a fact of life that a great many of us get turned on by other people-that the phenomenon is natural, if you will-there doesn't seem to be any point in getting upset about it."

In my own practice, it is far more common for one or both partners to admit that they are attracted to other people from the opposite sex when with me individually. Many will say, "I would never tell that to my partner." Since you read the chapter on sub-personalities (chapter 5), you can appreciate the following: While one of your partner's sub-personalities "only has eyes for you," there may be another sub-personality of hers that is attracted to someone else, or to some physical features that you do not possess, or to a certain kind of person who has a very different personality than you. Remember, you married an entire person, a person with complexity and a variety of sub-personalities. To summarize:

1. Accept the natural ambivalence you both have regarding marriage, spending time together, staying together, etc.

2. Go beyond your insecurities and embrace the sexuality of your partner; the parts of him that make you feel attractive and secure and the parts of him that may be attracted to other women. In my more than 25 years of clinical practice, I have seen this kind of sharing seem to *significantly decrease* the chances of infidelity and sometimes *increase* the sexual pleasure since it opens up the avenues of sexual expression.

If most people have ambivalence and can be attracted to others; and since extramarital affairs can be so destructive to the sacred bond of intimate relationships, there needs to be a way to bring one's sexual attraction and energy to one's partner. Sharing more of what and who is attractive to you with your partner without acting it out is the best way I know of solving this monogamy challenge. I am not saying that every time you have a desire or thought about someone else, you need to share it; but if you find that there is some part of you that feels a pull towards someone else and/or a pushing away from your partner, this may be the time to risk sharing more openly or, this could be discussed. If you are concerned about your partner's reaction, this would be a good time to seek a qualified marital/sex therapist who can help you and your partner navigate through these touchy feelings. The goal here is to make your emotional connection with each other more powerful than any sexual feeling. It would be ideal if each partner could get to the point like the wife of my acquaintance and say,

"Oh- you're attracted to someone else; you'll feel that way sometimes. Tell me more about that!" Some of you may not like this suggestion. However, creative monogamy just like other forms of interpersonal creativity often involves the willingness to endure uncomfortable feelings as you go from the egocentric position of "You should only have eyes for me" to the more mature position of "Keep sharing all of who you are, even the parts of you that make me feel uncomfortable." The paradox here is usually- *the more you accept this attraction to others and get creative with that part of your partner, the more attractive you become to him and the less energy he may have for the original target of his attraction.* In other words, use your partner's ambivalence or attraction to others as a way to deepen and broaden your own sexuality with him.

The Freedom of Being Married

Being unattached has certain freedoms. You can date who you please, have sex with whomever you want and answer to only yourself. Once married, you think of your partner's needs, and make time for her. Your intentions are to be loyal. My observation of "open marriages" is that they typically do not work. Having a committed sacred monogamous bond with your married partner seems to be the way to go in marriage. Only in the committed marital relationship do you have the freedom to practice creative monogamy. Marriage creates the interpersonal environment which is most conducive to risk sharing more of who you are, revealing the more "secretive," "hard to admit" parts of who you are. In other words, only in marriage or in a committed relationship do you have the freedom to be multidimensional and expand your definition of yourself in the presence of another person in an intimate way.

Most couples do not fully utilize this freedom they have in marriage. The more you express yourself and get curious about the multiple sub-personalities of your partner, the more you will grow into being the unique sexual partner you are capable of becoming.

10

Sex & Personal Growth

Sex and Its Different Agendas

As teenagers, we first start experimenting sexually to experience the feelings. These sexual feelings are pleasurable, exciting and consuming. The adolescent is not yet capable of true love because his sexual world is an egocentric world, the purpose of which is to have pleasure. If the girl is a source of pleasure, he "loves" her; if she stops being a source of pleasure for whatever reason, he stops "loving" her. This is age appropriate and totally normal as well as a necessary developmental step. These sexual feelings lead the adolescent to take the risks and begin forging ahead with the scary endeavor of boy meets girl. It gets him to overcome his fears and connect in sensual and sexual ways with the opposite sex.

Some use sex to be respected by peers such as the boy who exaggerates his sexual achievements so that other boys look up to him. This gives him a higher role in the pecking order giving him more respect, clout and power.

Young adults also use sex for feeling a sense of adequacy. "If I am good enough, people will be attracted to me." Also, from the very first kiss, they are looking for approval from the person they are kissing.

As a therapist, I have heard many sad stories of adults relaying their stories as adolescents and younger adults who had an absent opposite-sexed parent. In their attempt to feel secure and loved, they acted out sexually and were promiscuous. The physical contact made them feel safe and less alone in the world.

So far, I have mentioned four different "feeling states" that adolescents pursue with sexuality: pleasure, power, a sense of adequacy and a sense of security. As you are probably aware, grown up adults use sex to experience the same feelings as younger people. There is nothing inherently wrong with this. It feels good to feel secure and safe, adequate and "good enough", powerful and in control and to experience pleasurable sensual feelings. I highly recommend it. The problem is that as human beings, we are capable of so much more.

When I talked about Nate and Corinne earlier in the book, Nate was unconsciously using sex as a way to feel close and safe. He was using sex to relieve his feelings of abandonment having lost his mother and oldest sister at such young ages. His clingy touch turned off Corinne. This led to the downward negative spiral of him feeling abandoned once more, getting angrier and clingier and turning her off even more.

The mental imagery exercise I put him through helped him create a new agenda for having sexual and sensual touch with his wife. He could use his touch as a way of expressing his love and caring for his partner. This was his sexual expression coming from the heart as he perceived himself as a source of love that could offer his wife emotional nourishment at the moment of touching her. This was not only two people rubbing their bodies together. This was a mature and significantly more satisfying way of having sex.

Do not get me wrong. Having sex for all the other agendas is great and you should embrace those aspects of yourself and your partner that want to experience those pleasant feelings. We all want to feel pleasure, power, safe and adequate. In addition to these feeling states, you can tap into your ability to deeply care for your partner and convey this message of love through how you touch your partner. Try the imagery experience that Nate did on your own. Imagine the loving energy in the universe and breathe it in through the crown of your head, down into your heart. As you breathe out, imagine this loving energy going through your arms and hands and out your fingertips. Immerse yourself in this imagery and see your partner as a person who is loveable and needs your love. Touch her from this feeling state. I would guess that your touch may be different, softer perhaps. Your eyes would appear different to your partner and chances are that she will open up to the "vibration" you are emitting towards her.

I once saw a couple who were stuck in a sexual rut. He always wanted her to dress up sexy and naughty, getting aroused at her sexual power. Actually, they both enjoyed these role playing experiences. After a while, she started making excuses why she did not want to have sex with him. He insisted on them coming to therapy to deal with their decreasing sex. One of the statements she repeatedly said to me was that she just wanted "meat and potatoes sex." You can take that to mean that she wanted plain old boring sex. I took it to mean that she wanted to feel loved and cherished as opposed to just feel like an object used to arouse her husband.

Role playing can be wonderful for couples. It could be fun and exciting, just like any other enjoyable activity. This kind of playfulness can bring a couple closer together and keep the relationship exciting and fresh. I suggest the following:

Pay attention to your agenda. What do you want out of your sexual experience? You may choose to just go with your agenda. For example, you may want to have a quickie with your partner. As long as this is mutually agreed upon, enjoy yourselves. However, if you realize you have not had gentle, loving slower sex the last few times, you may choose to devote more time and loving attention to each other. Vary your sexual encounters; do not get stuck in a sexual rut.

Sex and Personal Growth

I believe we are here on earth to grow. It is obvious that babies grow, children grow and adolescents grow. They get taller, their muscles develop, and they learn how to walk, talk, dance and throw a football. They grow academically also. The 6 year old cannot grasp mathematical concepts like a 15 year old. Socially, the relationships that a 6 year old makes with peers are much different than that of a 15 year old. As you already know, we all grow physically, academically and socially.

As adults, we do not grow any taller, but social/emotional growth continues nonetheless. We are destined to grow. Marriages demand that we grow. Without growth, marriages die. I joke often how people call mental health clinicians "shrinks," but the truth is clients come in "shrunk"; they need to expand and grow beyond their self limitations. For example, the whole process of becoming a good listener requires expanding. Most of us childishly react to partner's negative feelings or feedback. In order to become good listeners, we need to learn to manage our impulse to cut in and correct. We need to develop patience to let our partner finish speaking and sensitivity to be in rapport with our expressing partner. As we practice the discipline and skill of listening we are growing emotionally and developing personally.

Your sexual relationship holds many opportunities for growth. Use your touch to convey love and deep caring. What follows are ways to use your sexual life to develop your spiritual qualities and reach your relationship potential.

Qualities You Can Develop in Your Sex Life with Your Spouse

Patience

1. Your partner will not always want to have sex when you want to. You need to accept your partner's differences. On the other

hand, your partner needs to be patient with your sexual needs as well.

2.   Lovemaking is not always the fluid, seamless dance that we see in fantasies or read about in romance novels. There can be misreads, requested changes in the kinds of touch, erection problems, interruptions from the kids, and other human "bumps in your sexual road." As an example, the man loses his erection for the first time and they both roll over and go to sleep, disappointed and frustrated. I have helped many of these couples just by suggesting that they do not end their lovemaking session after he loses an erection. They can enjoy the process of arousing the man after he has lost his erection so that he may gain his erection again. They can repeat this process many times if need be or if they want to. They learn to challenge the unconscious rule that everything works perfectly the first time. The focus can be more on being in the moment than performance.

Courage

As thinking humans, we are more complex than other living creatures. More primitive creatures have fears regarding their physical survival whereas in addition to physical survival fears, we have fears that threaten our psychological well being as well. We fear such emotional experiences as:

1.   rejection
2.   being inadequate/not pleasing
3.   abandonment
4.   being out of control
5.   losing our individuality/freedom

The sexual arena tests every individual in some or all of these areas. Rejection is always possible when you risk getting closer to another human being. There is always the possibility that you may not please your partner. Nobody can guarantee you that your partner will always be with you and will never leave or abandon you. There are many aspects about sex that are not in your control such as how your body will respond sexually; how your partner feels; if the kids are going to knock on the door, etc. As you get closer to your partner, it is true that you lose some of your individuality in a sense. As you merge physically with another, boundaries do blur. Also, as you get literally and metaphorically naked with your partner, you expose yourself; not just your outer body, but your inner world, including your desires, fears and needs.

Of course, as maturity deepens and you develop a sense of self, you can face these fears and develop more emotional muscle. Actually, due to the nature of sex with your partner, it may be the best arena to learn, become more self-aware, develop and grow. Relationships are not for cowards. Cowards stay in their self protective worlds unwilling to risk emotionally. The result of staying in your comfort zone is having relationships that lack passion. Courage opens the relationship to opportunities for creativity, pleasure and aliveness.

Fear of Rejection

In reality, rejection is an illusion. If your partner "rejects" you, she is expressing something about herself. In his book, "The Four Agreements," Carlos Ruiz states that people are living in their own dream whether they are asleep or awake. You are a character in your partner's dream. One of Ruiz's four healthy agreements is, "Don't take anything personally." Rather than take things personally and withdraw into a self-pitying emotional state, it will serve you better to get curious about what is behind your partner's "rejection." What is going on emotionally with her? What is making your partner say or do that particular thing that rejects you? What is she afraid of? The more you are willing to get rejected, and talk about the reason for the rejection, the more you will be able to stay connected to your partner and overcome whatever resistance there may be to getting close to each other.

Fear of being inadequate or not pleasing

If your partner is not pleased with something you do or do not do sexually, it is an opportunity to learn. Why do you think that you should know what pleases your partner without any mutual communication? Would you expect to dance a phenomenal salsa with your partner the first time? Or would you make mistakes like crazy, trip over each other, miss your connections and gradually get closer to a flow? Do not overrate adequacy and smoothness. Usually the couple who never gets frustrated, disappointed or flustered; who never has an awkward moment is a couple who lives far too safely and is headed for sexual boredom. Be courageous, create some awkwardness and have a sense of humor about yourself and you will have a juicy, passionate sexual relationship.

Fear of abandonment

There are many rewards for facing your fear of abandonment. There is not a person alive who has been loved perfectly or has never been abandoned in some way. It feels terrible to get hurt, abandoned or betrayed by someone who is important to you. If you take it personally and let it affect your own self- esteem or project the "abandoner" onto your partner, you can increase the chances of being abandoned. The self-fulfilling prophecy can work both positively and negatively. If you continue to act on your fear of abandonment, you will push your partner away in your attempt to protect yourself. You may say no to sex frequently or, during sex, you may not fully enjoy the present moment intimate experience. Your partner will inevitably get frustrated and tire of this behavior and there is a chance that he will pull away from you as well, whether it is emotionally or physically.

Ask yourself if there is any fear of abandonment holding you back from participating fully with your partner. If you notice any of this fear, take a few full relaxation breaths and allow your heart area to relax. Be willing to soften any bodily tension you feel. Say to yourself, "I am open to giving and receiving sexual energy with my partner." There are no guarantees in love and relationships; however the more courageous you are, the more you will be free to fully give of yourself to your partner. Your partner will feel more accepted and loved by you. Common sense says that if your partner feels this unabashed love and sexual energy, he will probably never want to leave. There are many paradoxes when discovering the nature of relationships and here is one of them: *The less you act on feeling abandoned, the less chance you will be abandoned.*

Fear of being out of control

Here is another paradox: *The more you can tolerate the feeling of being out of control, the more in control you are.* In the sexual arena of your relationship, you need to learn the art of letting go. Letting go involves letting go of all possible outcomes, fears. etc. and focusing on the pleasure of the moment. It means letting go of listening to the inner critic as was discussed in Chapter 9. It means risking showing your emotions and intensity. It may even mean yelling with pleasure! It may mean letting your body move in new, pleasurable ways. It may mean trying new positions or role playing just for fun. It may mean showing to your partner a part of yourself that he has not seen. If you are the type of person who tends to hold yourself in control, try going just a little past your edge of comfort. Possibly you can use the next sexual opportunity to let go a little more than before. I remember working with a man who did not allow himself to show his wife he was having pleasure even though he insisted he was. The wife mentioned that he did not even make a sound during roller coaster rides even though just like in sex, he claimed he was having a good time. Their homework assignment was to go to an amusement park and he was to get on a roller coaster with his wife just to practice hollering "Yeeeeehah!" as he went down the track. He did that and said that it felt good to give himself permission to sound on the outside how he felt on the inside. They began transferring that experience to the bedroom and had a lot of fun doing it.

Fear of losing one's individuality

We all have the need to be individuals and be our own unique selves. We need the freedom to express our inner feelings, desires, etc. A person who gives up his identity to accommodate another will feel empty, depressed and full of self-loathing. It is necessary and healthy to have boundaries, saying "Yes" to the things in life that nourish us and "No" to the things in life that are harmful or toxic to us. There are many people who do not have good boundaries and allow themselves to be abused or taken advantage of.

Whenever I have a man who has the symptoms of a low sexual drive, I look at the possible factors including physical factors such as medications and hormones that may be the reason for his lack of sexual desire. Also, I always ask about the relationship he had/has with his mother and more times than not, he has had an overbearing mother. The overbearing mother usually had no boundaries herself depending upon her son to take care of her emotional needs in some way. She also did not honor and respect the boundaries of her son. She did not treat him as an individual who had needs of his own, different than his mother. He was not allowed to disagree with his mother and go through the healthy defiance that children and adolescents usually go through. She needed her son to meet her emotional needs and be compliant to all her wishes.

The case already mentioned of Roger and Sarah illustrated this dynamic. Roger avoided sex because at an unconscious level, sex meant merging with another person. Roger's skin crawled when Sarah touched him because it triggered the smothering affect his mother's overbearing needs had on him. He saw his wife as his mother, needy and draining. His "crawling skin," as well as his years of avoiding sex with Sarah, were both symptoms to protect his individuality. He needed to find healthier, more mature ways to set boundaries and experiencing his own feelings, desires and sexuality. He needed to recognize that merging with his partner was not a threat to his individuality. You will read more on this subject in the next chapter.

Sensitivity

It is a given that some people are more sensitive than others. These people naturally tune in to people's needs and provide them with what they need. On the extreme end, these sensitive people may ignore their own needs and desires as they compulsively meet the needs of others. Some people are far less sensitive to the needs of others. Their ability to sense what others are experiencing and need is low. On the extreme end, these people are totally self-involved, trying to get their own needs met without compromise.

A flourishing sexual relationship requires reciprocity and mutuality. Assess yourself. Where are you on the continuum of sensitivity to others? Do you get easily affected by the pain of another to the point of you forget your own needs? Sexually, are you so tuned in to the needs of your partner that you do not ask yourself what you want or how you want to have sex with your partner even if it is different than your partner's preferences? If you answer yes to this question, get curious about your sexuality. Do you want to change or add something to your sexuality? Be willing to assert yourself even if your partner is not totally in favor of your request. "What am I feeling? What do I need from him? If I stopped worrying about his needs, what would I discover about myself?" You may have to experiment, asking him to try different types of touching, positions, kissing, etc. to see what feels the best to you. I encourage you to endure the initial discomfort of becoming more tuned in to yourself since it is so new and different than before. Simply put, it is taking your attention away from your partner and concentrating more on yourself.

If you are an under-sensitive person you need to take attention off you and onto your partner. This requires asking yourself questions such as, "What do I sense she is feeling right now?" "What do I think she wants right now?" Of course you can always ask her, which is a sensitive act in itself because the attention is on her. This can feel awkward and strange at first to the person who is not used to thinking about others. Thinking about the needs of others is a positive habit that can be cultivated over time. Write notes to yourself that remind you to get curious about your partner. Ask her how she would like to be touched. Forget about getting your needs met at least for now. As you practice this habit of focusing on her, you probably will be rewarded with a happy and loving spouse who would love nothing more than to please you as well.

There is no better classroom for learning to be sensitive than in the bedroom with your partner. Here are some ways to increase your sensitivity with your partner in the bedroom.

MEN

1. Look into your partner's eyes. Turn your thoughts away from yourself and notice your partner.

2. For the moment, relax all your strivings and stop trying to get anything from your partner. Just be with her.

3. Remember that she has feelings and desires just like you and many of them may be different than yours at this moment. Imagine what she might want from you right now. Of course you can always ask her.

4. Give her what she needs that is possible for you to give to her right now. See her needs as important as your own.

5. Change your touch, slow down, experience your hands as conduits of sexual love. Change how you touch; notice her verbal and nonverbal signals. Is it more pleasurable, less pleasurable? If it seems less pleasurable, adjust your touch again. Ask her how it feels and how she would like to be touched.

WOMEN

1. Look into your partner's eyes. Turn your thoughts away from yourself and notice your partner.
2. Remember that he has feelings and desires just like you and many of them may be different than yours at the moment. Imagine what he wants from you. Ask or listen to your intuition about this.
3. Give him what he needs that is possible for you to give. See his needs as important as your own.
4. Notice what arouses him. Be as willing as possible to stretch outside your comfort zone to pleasure your man.

Creativity

Sex with your mate is not unlike any other creative pursuit. What is wonderful about any creative pursuit is that you have many choices and can make an impact by bringing your involvement, energy and intention to the creative process. Of course, if you want beautiful results, there are guidelines. In music, you cannot just play any notes you want; the notes have to come together in some harmonic, systematic way. However, within that chordal system, whether it is jazz, rock and roll, or classical music, there are an infinite number of choices. In painting, the artist needs to have some structure with the brushstrokes to create the beauty and/or the emotional impact he wants to create.   Usually, the artist or musician has already learned his craft and realizes that the more skill he has, the more unlimited his ability will be to create.

Likewise, sexuality with your partner has to follow guidelines of sensitivity. You cannot just do whatever you want.   However, the more sensitive you are, and the more you learn about your partner's sexual and emotional needs, the more uninhibited you both can be in creating "beautiful music together."   There are so many ways to touch, kiss, embrace, rub, talk, imagine, thrust, penetrate and receive in the bedroom with your partner. As in music and art, the advantage often goes to the couple who has spent the most time attending to the sexually creative process. This is why older couples often report that they have far better sex now than when they were younger. Of course these are the couples who have done their sexual homework devoting time and attention to each other throughout their relationship.

In summary, sex with your partner is a rich arena for personal growth. There is much fodder here to develop your patience, courage, sensitivity and creativity. Why not make your sex life a vehicle to develop these qualities? There are two great benefits to this. One is that these developing qualities transfer to other areas of your life and you can have more of what you want in those areas as well. Secondly, as you develop these qualities, you can continue experiencing greater levels of your sexual potential and thereby leading to greater pleasure and emotional connection between you and your mate. An upward movement is created that can continue for the rest of your married life.

11

Receiving in the Bedroom

The old adage that it is better to give than to receive may be true in some areas but in terms of relationship I think they are equally important. The problem is that if we don't know how to receive, it is really hard to truly give. People that do not know how to receive well are not giving from that adult inside of them. They are usually giving from the parent part that is trying to manage or help other people or trying to give from the child part who wants approval. When the intent of giving is to manage and control or get approval, the "giver" ends up being resentful and can burn out because he is not coming from his truest desires. On the other hand, adult-to-adult giving and receiving is between two "equals" who are connecting, opening to each other's love and mutual pleasure.

One of the best ways to begin being aware of your ability to receive and how much you are letting love and good feelings enter your experience is to notice your bodily tension. Ask yourself, "When my partner touches me, am I relaxed?" "Is my chest closed, is my stomach tight? When I kiss, is my mouth soft and open, or am I tight? Is my jaw clenched?" Whenever there is tension in intimacy, it is automatic resistance to receiving from your partner and being open. As I discussed earlier regarding opening up to your partner, in order for you to have a better sex life you need to learn how to be tuned into what is going on in your body. Only then, can you intervene in your automatic fear patterns and shift from pushing your partner's gifts away to allowing them into your experience.

Resistance to Pleasure

Place your two hands together in front of you, palm to palm. Press each hand into each other so that there is equal pressure and the hands stay in the same place. Feel the resistance in your hands to the force being exerted by the other hand. That feeling of resistance felt in your hands can be similar to the feelings felt in other parts of your body as well. When you are about to do something that you don't want to do, you can feel the resistance in the form of tension or contraction in your body. It is as if you are opposing the "doing" of the activity by your resistance.

Some people are highly resistant to sexual pleasure. This resistance usually takes the form of unconscious tension in different parts of the body such as the stomach, heart and face areas. This resistance to receiving sexually is actually trying to serve the person in some way (as discussed below) even though the costs to the sexual relationship are high. There are five themes that I have discovered people play out over and over in their lives that can greatly contribute to difficulty to sexual (and non-sexual) receiving.

The Five Themes that Contribute to Sexual Resistance

1. Survival vs. non-survival: This person could have grown up in a chaotic home where survival was the main event. There was no space for meeting each other's emotional needs. Maybe there was violence in the home or other kinds of abuse or neglect. This theme of survival continues through the person's life

including in the current committed relationship. When life is about survival; in other words-just making it through another day without being harmed, allowing receiving from another person is not even on the agenda. As mates, they are as uncomfortable receiving sexual pleasure as they are receiving other forms of emotional nourishment such as getting compliments, or being on the receiving end of romantic gestures.

2. <u>Shame vs. goodness:</u> This person learned anti-sexual messages growing up. This could be due to being brought up in a fundamentally religious home. She also could have been molested and associates sex with shame. This person is constantly striving to "not be bad." Sexuality brings up shame and this leads to tremendous resistance to sex and pleasure.

3. <u>Power vs. powerlessness:</u> This person has learned to be overly independent and was rewarded in some way for this excessive independence. She has built up unconscious walls to avoid the vulnerability of feeling pleasure from another human being. Instead, for her, the relationship is about either being one up (dominant position) or one down (submissive position). She chooses to avoid feelings of powerlessness at the expense of experiencing the joys of mutual pleasuring.

4. <u>Abandonment vs. guaranteed love and acceptance:</u> This person has experienced significant loss and/or abandonment and is protecting herself from feeling another loss. If she were to allow herself to feel sexual pleasure, especially intense sexual pleasure sensations, she would need him more and therefore be setting herself up for a major loss in the event that he left her someday.

5. <u>Adequacy vs. inadequacy:</u> Life in and out of the bedroom is one constant performance after another. Sexuality and sensual pleasures are perceived as high stakes risks to being good

enough. This person chooses to avoid feeling incompetent over the joys of mutual pleasuring.

Overcoming the 5 Themes of Resistance:

If you know yourself to be significantly resistant to receiving sexual pleasure, see if one or more of these 5 themes relate to you. Realize that you have unconsciously restricted yourself sexually and probably in other areas of your life as well. Do not judge yourself because there are psychological reasons why people adopt certain themes in their life. Usually it is because they were deprived of something psychologically important in their lives. The person whose theme is survival probably lived in a home where survival seemed threatened. The person whose theme is shame vs. goodness was made to feel ashamed by the big people in her life back then. This follows for all five themes. The adopted themes are attempted solutions to one or more interpersonal or other life problems. The problem is that these attempted solutions have helped create other interpersonal problems, mainly in the form of closing off to love and sexual pleasure.

The good news is that once you are aware of the theme(s) that is holding you back sexually, you can begin to challenge your own limited cognitive perceptions. For example, you may begin to see that your life is not at all about survival. Or you may realize that in your attempt to be adequate, you have missed the understanding that you already are enough as you are. In all of these themes, you hopefully realize that your constant attempts to achieve security, goodness, power, guaranteed love and acceptance or adequacy are like the proverbial "dog chasing its tail." The only real solution to these themes is to step out of them entirely and affirm that you are already that which you have frantically tried to be. In other words, you already have security, power and the rest. Realize that the only thing that made you feel the lack of these things is that you had beliefs from the past that you have long held onto. Let your new awareness sink in.

The next step is to challenge those beliefs by experimenting receiving from your mate. As you allow yourself more pleasure, there is an excellent chance that your resistance will flare up even more strongly than before. You are risking and playing with old defense mechanisms. Be patient with yourself but don't give in to the old themes. Your partner and your sexual relationship with your partner is a great training ground to increase your capacity to feel loved, cherished and pleasured.

The Importance of Dependency

I worked with a couple named Sharon and Edward. Edward is an attorney and Sharon is a psychotherapist, both around 50 years old. As a child, Edward's parents were extremely busy running a butcher shop in New York. He was provided for quite adequately, but had little if any emotional attention from his busy, hard-working parents. As an adult, Edward had been through some difficult relationships and always was the one pursuing and initiating and trying to make things happen. He went out of his way to please the date, girlfriend or partner whether it was through acts of kindness, gifts or lots of affection. Each of the relationships ended up in the female ending the relationship. His theme was abandonment vs. guaranteed love and acceptance.

Sharon had been in a series of relationships before she met Edward where she always felt smothered by the man she was with and would ultimately break up with them. During one of our sessions Edward said, "Every time that I sit down with Sharon, I need to right away put my arm around her and hug her. She is not always thrilled with my 'moves'." As with some couples, old patterns re-surface and get reenacted over and over again. Edward felt like he had to smother her as a way to feel close, and Sharon pushed him away.

I asked him to sit on his hands when he was with her. He was not to touch or put his arm around her. Being the litigator that he was, he stood up and said, "That's not who I am. I'm the kind of guy who is affectionate and I want to put my arms around my partner." I said that I understood that, and then asked him if he had ever experienced someone going out of her way for him; had he experienced someone loving and caring for him with him being at the receiving end? And he quickly said, "No I never have." Then I said, "This is not about changing who you are, this is about the opportunity to learn how to allow another person to come to you." He said, "So you want me to sit on my hands? I replied, "Yes." He said, "Well what if she doesn't come to me?" I said, "We'll have to find that out won't we?" That week, he literally sat on his hands. Not only did Edward get to have the new experience of being the object of his wife's affections, but Sharon was happy because she had the opportunity to make the first move towards him for a change.

We depend upon water for drinking, food for eating and air for breathing. Our emotional needs have to be met as well. We all have an independent and self-reliant aspect of our inner nature. At the same time, we have a dependent part of our nature and in order to have a healthy relationship, we need to be able to access both aspects of our inner nature. Dependency is not the same as over-dependency. Over-dependency is when a person is doing nothing for himself. Healthy dependency involves being self-reliant and self-soothing as we have discussed but also, being able to trust others to be there for us. Remember that to bring the "giving" part out of your partner, you need to perceive your partner as someone you can count on. If you are seeing your partner as someone you cannot count on, you are treating him that way as well and you are helping to maintain the same dynamic as before.

Ask Yourself, "What Do I Want?"

Upon asking some of my clients what they want, there are those who do not have a clue how to answer that question. Try it yourself. Ask yourself, "What do I want from my partner?" Allow yourself to have wants. If you have trouble coming up with an answer to that question, stop thinking too hard about it. Notice whatever comes up. It does not have to be anything huge. It could be a hug, a kiss or five minutes of listening to you about something that is troubling you. Remember, if you are not asking that question and you are not learning to receive, you are not going to be as giving as you think you are. It is always easier to give more fully that which you allow yourself to receive.

I'd Like to Go for a Walk

I had a client named George, who at 6'8" was one of my tallest clients. He was also one of the most gentle and passive as well. He was in a group session; the purpose was for participants to break free of fear and accelerate self-development. Each week, all the participants had home assignments that were designed to challenge them, to help them overcome their fears, and ultimately to increase their happiness. At one session, I asked George what he wanted from his wife that she does not know about. His comment, which was not at all surprising, was "I don't know", and he followed up with, "I want my partner to be happy."

I pressed George some more and he finally said, "I would like to go for a walk with my wife." I asked him, "When was the last time you had a walk with your wife?" He said, "We've never gone for a walk." I said "Your homework assignment for this week is to go for a walk. He replied, "Ok." For George this was a challenging assignment that created anxiety for him. At the next group meeting I checked in with George about his assignment. He said, "Yeah, I did my homework." Another group member asked how he enjoyed the walk with his wife, and he said that they did not go on a walk. Here is the dialogue that followed:

George: I asked her to go for a walk and she said, "Well, I'm kind of busy." So that was that!

Todd: On a scale of 1 to 10, 1 being- I can go for a walk but it's not that big of a deal and 10 is- I really, really, really, really want to go for a walk, what is it?

George: It's a 10.

Todd: Well, then what you need to do is go up to your wife and you say, "I want to go for a walk" and if she says she's too busy, then gently touch her on the shoulders and say "No, you don't understand," and give her the four 'reallys': "I really, really, really, really want to go for a walk," and see what happens.

I asked him to practice this and role play with the group with each one of us playing the role of his wife.

At the following group session, I ask him how he did with the assignment. George said, "Yeah, I asked her to go for a walk, and she said she was too busy, and so I did as you said, I touched her shoulders and said- 'no you don't understand, I really, really, really, really want to go for a walk', and she said 'Oh, ok, let's go then." And then every day since then, she has been asking me if I want to go for a walk today!" George was delighted at his new revelation- he could express what he wanted and also let his wife know how intensely he wants it. And he may even get what he wants!

Healthy Selfishness in the Bedroom- Bridget and Michael

Bridget and Michael came into my office. Bridget was very upset with Michael because she caught Michael with his hand in his pants viewing some pornography and yet he would never initiate sex with her. She made the comment to me, "He is so selfish", which I responded back, "No, I think the problem is that he's not selfish enough." She got angry with me for saying that, and I said, "Let me explain." How often does he come to you and say "Honey, let's make love and let's try it this way, touch me here or touch me there or say sweet nothings in my ear?" She replied, "Never, he's never done that; but it would be great if he did." I said "Yes it would, and that's being selfish. It is important to distinguish between the words selfish and self-absorbed. Self absorbed is not a very good thing. Selfish is a good thing. If your husband is selfish, he is asking for what he wants and he's involved with you and letting you be involved with him. Self absorbed is what he does when he's masturbating with his pornography. He's not connecting with you. You're not involved in the process. He's not dealing with you on an adult-to-adult basis; that's the little child inside that is running him and it's his way of getting his sexual needs met, rather than an adult-to-adult way of getting his needs met."

We all need to begin to "take up more space in the relationship" as our partner needs to acknowledge who we are and make room for us to be who we are. Otherwise, we end up having bastardized versions of dependency, such as chemical dependency, food dependency, extra-marital affairs, sexual dependency, and other unhealthy forms of self-absorbed dependency. Are you going to be healthily selfish or unhealthily self-absorbed?

The Relationship Between Selfishness and Generosity

Fast forward Michael and Bridget's relationship after he takes the chance to ask her to make love to him a certain way and she enthusiastically and positively responds. He is finding out in one small way that what he wants counts. How do we react when we feel like what we want counts to that person? How do we feel about that person? Typically and understandably, we feel good about that person. We often times have a desire to give back; it is only natural. When people treat us well, it's easier to treat people well. It's just that simple. Michael began experiencing asking and receiving more from his wife and predictably he became far more attentive and caring to Bridget.

The Case of Paul and Christine

Paul wanted to have sex with Christine more often and he was very frustrated with her resisting his advances. She was bitter towards him because of his consistent continuous sexual advances. Eventually he gave up trying to initiate sex and they had a sexless marriage, because he couldn't take it any more. He wanted out of the relationship. When he called me, they were just about to separate.

When they came in as a couple, I ask Christine what is it that she would want, or what would have to happen for her to want to make love to him more. Her response to me was "I just wish he wouldn't be so needy." I told her that sometimes what we judge in others are aspects we need to develop more in ourselves, In her case, it may be helpful to see if she is not being "needy enough" (to use her language). I asked her again what she may need other than her partner to be less needy. By this time, you may predict what she said. "I don't know. I guess I just want to not feel the pressure of having to have sex with him." When a person answers the question, '*What do I want?*' with something negative, she is not really saying what she wants. She is saying what she does not want. It was clear that Christine was not tuned in to what it was that she wanted from Paul.

It was very important for Christine to learn how to become healthily selfish. Again, it began with her understanding and recognizing that she approached sex as if it was all about her husband. She never looked at sex as something in which she could get pleasure. It may seem obvious that sex is about pleasure, but many people approach the bedroom as a place where they have to service others. She came from a family where she had an absent father for most of her life, and a mother who had mental illness, so she had to grow herself up prematurely and be like a little adult. Her dependency needs had to be shut off to survive and make sense of growing up in her family of origin. She grew up to be a very attractive woman, and Paul and Christine enjoyed their sexuality in the courting stage and early part of their relationship. Shortly after marriage, all her wanting to have sex just shut off. She became the manager, the doer and the mother of not only the kids and the step kids, but of her husband. She seemed to shift from being "mother" who has a needy "son" to "daughter" who needed to please her demanding "father". The only way to shift to an adult to adult pattern in the bedroom was to learn how to be healthily selfish.

The project ahead of her was to find out what it was that she wanted and to begin looking at sex as something for her. First, she needed to become more aware of the two themes of resistance that were operating: Survival vs. Non-survival and Power vs. Powerlessness. She became aware of how much of the time her psyche experienced life as a test for survival even though her survival was in no apparent danger. She realized that most of her waking time was filled up with worrying about her children and step-children, problems in the world, etc. She gave herself permission to have moments where she gave up the psychological fight for survival and made room for self care and enjoying her life. She also recognized her fear of being powerless and how she hardened herself to protect herself from feeling this powerlessness. Little by little, what she started to recognize is that she can have boundaries and that this was true, healthier power. She needed to feel like she could say no to certain things and yes to others. In a nutshell, that is what boundaries are- saying yes to what you want and no to what you do not want. So I told her that it's ok to say no to some things, but let's start to say yes to things that you may want. Instead of looking at sex as giving to him, the key was for her to ask herself '*What is it that I want sexually?*' She had to continually challenge herself to not slip into the mode of '*I have to service him*' and more in terms of sex is for me as well. In the beginning of treatment with this couple, we made sex all about her needs, and Paul's job was to respond to her needs, and he understood the necessity of that temporary one-sidedness. She started to realize that she can be touched in ways that she likes and she began using sex as a way of feeling pleasure. The more she acknowledged her own needs for touch the less she judged him for his needs for touch.

Paul and Christine eventually made a contract they both felt comfortable with. He vowed to listen more and yield more to her wishes and pace of sex together. She was willing to meet his wish to not go more than 48 hours without sexual activity. As long as she feels this is her choice as well as his, this will work. If she ever starts to feel "obligated," changes need to be made either to her way of thinking, their "contract" or both.

Another Example Of Using Sex as a Boundary vs.

Developing Boundaries in Sex

Carl and Nadine had not touched in seven years; no holding hands, no hugging, not even a peck on the cheek. Nadine refused any physical connection whatsoever. She claimed she liked her husband but could not touch him. Carl was a recovering alcoholic who had been going to AA for seven years, the same amount of time as the non-touching had been going on. Carl was very frustrated. Nadine had no idea why she rejected him physically and they both felt stuck. One session, I asked them to kiss each other that following week, just once. I did not know what would happen but I was curious what they would do with that request. They came in the following week and had not kissed. I gave them the same assignment again hoping the nuisance of having to tell me they had not done it again would motivate Nadine to overcome her resistance and do the assignment. The next week, they did kiss. However, Carl said that her mouth was so tight during their kiss that "you would not be able to stick a pin in her mouth."

I decided to do some hypnotherapy with Nadine and see if she could have greater access to her resistance. I asked Carl to wait in the waiting room. I helped Nadine relax and then asked her to imagine Carl coming towards her. I asked her to allow her face to soften and open her mouth gently as Carl gently pressed his lips onto hers. I asked her to continue to soften and relax and let his kiss penetrate her experience. At that point, she exclaimed, "UHHH" in a way that expressed aversion and disgust. I asked her what was going on and she said that she felt disgust as she imagined his passionate kiss. At that point, my instincts told me to run out and get Carl from the waiting room. When he sat down, I asked her to tell Carl what happened. She was concerned that his feelings would be hurt, but I said that I thought he could handle it. She told him about her feelings of disgust. Carl replied, "Well no kidding, I knew that already. I feel your disgust; you haven't touched me for 7 years! But why? Why are you disgusted?"

Nadine first said that she did not know, but then she seemed to go a bit deeper inside of herself as when in hypnosis earlier and said, "You know, when you were drinking, you asked me to do sexual things that I did not want to do. I hated myself for doing those things." She got more emotional as she said, "My father never molested me, but he dominated me and did not care about what I felt or wanted. I think I felt the same way with you when you drank and we had sex. I think when you got sober; I made a promise to never feel dominated again. I was not going to feel ashamed or ever compromise myself again." Notice the two themes of Shame vs. Goodness and Power vs. Powerlessness.

There was the obvious payoff for not touching. By not having any kind of physical relationship with Carl, she could avoid feeling her shame as well as her powerlessness (as she felt with her father). Nadine had made an unconscious decision to set a boundary by *not having sexual or even non-sexual physical contact with her husband.* As you can imagine, this was an emotional and enlightening experience for both partners.

From this point, Carl and Nadine learned about how to set boundaries, be healthily selfish and give and receive during lovemaking. She was able to be true to herself and have a sexual life with Carl simultaneously. She could say "No" to him and she could say "Yes" to him. It was her choice and she had the freedom to choose in any instant whether she was sexually connecting with him or not. She could even initiate her own ideas and ask Carl to accommodate to her wishes!

This is a common problem with couples. What is going on in your relationship? Is sex being used as a boundary or are you both learning to develop boundaries in sex? Practice asking for what you want and be sensitive to what your partner wants. Self-soothe when you do not get what you want and give permission to yourself to say no to your partner if that maintains your own integrity.

A Useful Definition of Masculinity and Femininity

These words are thrown around a lot and there is much confusion to what it means to be masculine and feminine. We all have masculine and feminine qualities. The masculine is the part of us that can have an impact on others and <u>pen</u>etrate the world or another person in some way. The <u>pen</u>is <u>pen</u>etrates and symbolically speaking, we penetrate when we make things happen and allow others to receive us and be affected by our actions. The feminine in us receives just like the vagina. It is the part of us that can open up and allow the world or others to affect us. The masculine in us gives; the feminine in us receives. The masculine in us is in a state of action and doing; the feminine in us is in a state of being and allowing. Men who are too much in their masculine have negative side affects such as premature aging and early heart problems as well as deprivation of the joy of "stopping to smell the roses." Women who are too much in their feminine may lack skills to make it in the world which can lead to becoming too dependent on men sometimes resulting in trapping themselves in toxic relationships. They can live too much in the shadow of their spouses and not find their own way and their own individual path. We need some sort of balance to thrive in this world. We as individuals are all unique and relationships are all unique, which means that balance for one individual or couple may look and feel different than balance for another individual or couple.

Having said that, for the majority of couples, in order to have a long, hot marriage, men need to feel masculine in relationship to their wives and women need to feel feminine in relationship to their husbands. When a women needs to do too much, manage and be overly responsible, her feminine and sexual hormones eventually shut off. Likewise, men need to feel that they make a positive impact on their wives. They need to feel their masculine power, not in a dominating sort of way, but in a way that makes a positive difference in the emotional lives of their female partners. Mother/son dynamics in relationships where the wife has to manage and make up for the husband's childish egocentricity usually lead to a sexual dead end. The wife in the "mother" role is way too much in her masculine and the husband is emasculated. I am not saying that she emasculates him. The unconscious dance they do leads to one or both partners desexualizing because of the fading and distorting of the masculine and feminine energies.

I have found that the healthiest of couples are fluid in their masculine and feminine roles, yet, sexually the men live from their masculine core and the women live from their feminine core. For example, asking your wife to dress sexy and naughty and be in her sexual power is great but you need to realize that this is a masculine role, (as funny as that may seem) in the way I define masculine. *She is having the affect on you.* Healthy couples can play with this and enjoy it thoroughly. However, what makes her feel sexual in the long term, is the feeling of being able to depend on her husband, to feel loved and cherished by him and to be able to open up to his loving touch, words and energy. Likewise, men can enjoy experiencing melting into their women's strong sexuality, but also need to feel their ability to "sweep their partner off their feet" and to love their female partners so totally and passionately that the wives melt into their sexual energy.

Before complaining about your wife's lack of femininity, look to see how you are contributing to it. Are you developing a lifestyle with your wife that allows her to just "be" at periods of time or is she in her masculine all day long? If she is in her masculine, do something to evoke her feminine. If you do not, do not expect her to want to be sexual and open with you. Remember- be creative in your relationship. Think like this: If there is a problem here, how am I contributing to it and what can I do to change it. Do not blame yourself, but look for ways you are responsible and have the intention to make a difference.

Before complaining about your husband's lack of masculinity, look to see how you are contributing to it. Are you the type that has a hard time trusting anyone; letting others do for you? Do you allow yourself to stop and smell the roses or are you doing and managing all day long? Will you allow yourself to shift gears in the presence of your husband and be in your feminine energy? Again, do not blame yourself; just look for ways to slow down and allow him to be there for you.

As you become more aware of your ability to bring something different out of you to evoke something different out of your spouse, you are in an increasingly more influential position to create a warm, loving, hot, passionate marriage. Enjoy the process, revel in the small gains and be patient with yourself and your mate. As you evolve past the unconscious, reactive habits of your ancestors, you are laying down a healthier framework for the generations to come. Remember, we are trailblazing in this area of relationships. Recently, someone asked me if it is really possible to have a long, hot marriage. I said, "Absolutely, as long as we do something different than what our ancestors did." There is no substitute for courage, vision and creativity. Do not look back; instead look forward. We have not even scratched the surface of our relationship potential. It is definitely time to get started.

Exercises to Break Through Sexual Resistance

1. We usually deal with resistance by avoiding the feeling, activity or person we have resistance to. This keeps us in our comfort zone. Like the example of Roger and Sarah, you need to be willing to go outside your comfort zone to experience more emotional and physical closeness with your partner. Put yourselves in a sexual situation or position that you usually avoid. The goal here is greater awareness of obstacles to sexuality. Begin with one of you touching the other. If negative feelings emerge in your partner, ask about it. "What exactly are you feeling or experiencing? Where does that come from? Did something happen in your past to account for this reaction? What have I done or what am I doing presently that contributes to your reaction? What are you thinking about? Invite your partner to be as revealing as possible. When she is finished, ask if you can resume the sexual behavior or touching that you did before. Respect your partner's answer. Most importantly, be kind, sensitive and patient.

2. An individual exercise you can do to be more sexually free is to "pretend" to be more sexual than you were in the past. You may want to move erotically in front of the mirror or do a striptease. When you feel more confident you can do this in front of your partner. The key here is to claim more of your sexuality. You can also buy lingerie or go to a sex shop and see if there is anything that appeals to you that you could try with your spouse.

3. Role play with your partner. Be willing to take on a role that is not typical for you. Be creative and have fun with it.

Exercises to Increase Healthy Dependence

1. Ask yourself, "What do I want sexually from my partner?" It has to be something that would allow you to feel more loved, pleasured, emotionally nourished and/or cherished. Once you come up with your answer, imagine your partner as capable of giving that to you. Forget the past and start a new and original story for the two of you. If he does not come through immediately, do not let him off the hook. Let him know how important it is for you to have whatever it is you want and let him know how much you need him. Only with patience, time and imagination can you truly find out what somebody is truly capable of.

2. Lie on your partner's lap and let her touch your face. Notice any resistance or bodily tension, and allow yourself to relax into her touch as much as you can. For this exercise, it is one-way giving. You need not reciprocate.

3. Let your partner hug you without hugging back. Keep your arms at your sides. Feel the one-way hug as love and emotional nurturing. Thank him for his love.

4. Say the words, "I trust you and I can count on you. I can relax in your loving arms. I forgive you for the hurt I experienced from your actions and I now let you love me again." Of course, change, add and delete the words to make it resonate with your experience. Do not wait to feel that way in order to say those words. Sometimes we have to act or speak first to bring up the feelings we would like to experience.

Exercises to Realign the Masculine and Feminine

Suggestion: Take a ballroom dance class or swing class with your partner. The man gets to lead and initiate; the woman gets to follow and respond.

For the Men

1. Be romantic. (Look at the exercises in Chapter 8) This is a guaranteed way to bring out the femininity of your spouse.
2. Set up a date. Do all the work. Get the babysitter. Maybe even surprise her with the date.
3. Ask what you can do with the children or around the house so that your wife can get a break and have personal time to do whatever she wants to do with her leisure time.
4. Be a sensitive lover. Make sure that you initiate lovemaking at least some of the time. This lets her know that you desire her.

For the Women

1. Put on a sexy dress or wear lingerie to bring out your own feeling of femininity.
2. Be aware of how willing or unwilling you are to have him be strong for you. (Often when the female complains that he is not there for her, or that she "wears the pants in the house," both people are contributing to this unhappy dynamic. He may not be attentive or giving enough nurturance to her satisfaction, and simultaneously-she may be uncomfortable with being the vulnerable one who needs something from the partner. It is very common to pick a mate that keeps us miserable but also in familiar territory. It requires courage to be open to something new in one's partner or oneself). Allow yourself to lean on him in a way you may not usually do. Let him know that you need him at times to feel loved and cherished.

3. Show appreciation for the masculine things he does for you. Men tend to do more when they are noticed for what they do.

The exercises in this chapter as well as those described throughout the book are tremendous catalysts for developing and maintaining the long, hot marriage. We know that the benefits of going to the gym to work out only happen if we do the workouts consistently and over a long period of time. These exercises work the same way. Do them consistently. There is no limit to how much love, pleasure and joy can pass between couples who are on this voyage.

12

Concluding Thoughts

As you continue your journey on the road to the long, hot marriage, it may be helpful to keep in mind the following:

1. A relationship is an adventure. Treat it is as such. Experiment with new perceptions of your partner. Courageously share your feelings. Listen to hers. Explore new sexual behaviors and approaches.

2. There are tremendous variances in temperament, desires and preferences among each gender; however, it is safe to say that men and women are different when it comes to sex. Respect and nurture each others differences. There is truth to what John Gray says- Men are from Mars and Women are from Venus. (Having said that, I have seen exceptions to this pattern in my practice. Sometimes I have seen men who need more feelings and sensitivity. I have seen women who are not as much into foreplay and connecting and have much higher libido than their male counterparts). We cannot afford to judge each other; we need to understand our differences and stretch and grow to meet each others needs.

3. If there are problems sexually, do not overlook non-relationship factors. Low sexual desire as well as arousal and orgasm difficulties could be caused by various physical/biological factors such as hormonal factors, medication side effects, chronic illness and the natural aging process. Talk to your doctor if you believe that any of these physiological factors are interfering with your sex life. The key is to be realistic and flexible in your lovemaking. (See # 6 below)

4. Regarding medication- if any medication includes the side effect of "may make you drowsy" it could affect libido, arousal and/or orgasmic capability. Blood pressure medications, antidepressants, antihistamines, anti-anxiety medications and sleep aids all can have sexual side effects. The good news is that improved medications with fewer side effects are coming out. For example, even though antidepressants can affect libido, some of the more recent studies show that significant sexual side effects are in a minority of the people taking some of the newer medications. Also, doctors can combine medications. The popular serotonin reuptake inhibitors such as Lexipro, Selexa and Zoloft can sometimes be combined with other antidepressants such as Wellbutrin that work with the chemical neurotransmitters-dopamine and norepinephrine. This combining can sometimes reduce sexual symptoms. Cymbalta, another antidepressant, increases the activity of both serotonin and norepinephrine and I have not seen too many sexual side effects with this drug. Talk to your doctor about options that best suit your needs that can take into consideration both your mental health and sexual needs.

5. Older couples are usually quite capable of having wonderful sex well into their 80s and even 90's. There may be the need for more physical stimulation and more foreplay in general. Since testosterone levels go down in both men and women as they get

older, it may be prudent to get your testosterone checked with a simple blood test if you are having desire or arousal difficulties. Women also need to pay attention to their other hormone levels such as estrogen and progesterone. Experienced gynecologists will guide you to make the best choices regarding the emotionally charged topic of hormone replacement therapy. My bias is that as people get older, they should do whatever they can to enjoy their sex life as long as there are not other serious dangers to their health.

6. Creating the "Long, Hot Marriage" has less to do with what you do and more about how you do it. Creating a pleasurable and loving intensity between you is the most important thing. I remember seeing a short documentary during my training in sexuality at UCLA. The short story involved an ambulatory woman married to a quadriplegic man. He had no sensations in his genital area. In order to make love, it took some preparation. She had to take his braces off and lift him one limb at a time out of the wheelchair onto the bed. Once in bed, they touched each other. He needed to use his forearm and elbow to touch her in her erogenous zones. He had developed sensitivity in his chest area midway between his nipples and shoulders. They were fully in the present moment, totally engaged with giving and receiving pleasure. This was truly a hot encounter that had no intercourse and none of the typical ways people physically connect while making love.

7. Take good care of yourself. Being a creatively sexual partner requires you to be in as good health and shape as possible. Exercise regularly, eat healthily and get enough sleep. Strive for balance in your life and do not overdrive your life.

8. Remember to make time and space for your sexual relationship. Guard against your to do list taking over your intimate relationship. It is a common affliction, but there is no need for

you to fall into that trap. There may be days where you have only minutes to be intimate and other days where you have more time. Be consistent. Don't let too much time go by without quality time where you both attend to each other and let everything else recede to the background of your mind and life.

9. All committed relationships have an ebb and flow. There are times when life situations come together in a way that makes it easier to have enjoyable and loving intimate encounters with your partner. Take full advantage of these times. At other times, life may be more challenging whether it is due to health, financial, time or transition issues. Do the best you can during these "ebb" times to connect with your partner, even though you may need to lower your expectations. Allow these cycles of life and relationship to happen and flex as best you can with them.

The Resources and Bibliography section that follows lists extremely helpful products and experiences that could aid you in your own personal development as a partner or could help you both as a couple. Everything listed I either personally read, experienced or am very familiar with their work.

Bibliography

Barbach, L. *For Each Other: Sharing Sexual Intimacy.* New York: Signet, 2001

Beavers, W.R. *Successful Marriage: A Family Systems Approach to Couples Therapy.* New York: W.W. Norton & Company, 1985

Carnes, P. *Out of the Shadows: Understanding Sexual Addiction.* 3rd ed. Center City, Minn.: Markham: Hazeldon, 2001

Deida, D. *The Way Of the Superior Man: A Spiritual Guide to Mastering the Challenges of Women, Work and Sexual Desire.* Louisville, KY.: Sounds True, 2004

Friel, John C. and L. D. Friel. *The 7 Best Things (Happy) Couples Do.* Deerfield Beach, FL.: Health Communications, Inc., 2002

Gray, John. *Men Are From Mars, Women Are From Venus: A Practical Guide for Improving Communication and Getting What You Want in Your Relationships.* New York: HarperCollins Publishers, Inc., 1992

Gray, John. *Why Mars and Venus Collide: Improving Relationships by Understanding How Men and Women Cope Differently With Stress.* New York: HarperCollins Publishers, Inc., 2008

Hendrix, H. *Getting the Love You Want- A Guide for Couples.* New York: Henry Holt @ Co., 1988

Lerner, Harriet *The Dance of Connection: How to Talk to Someone When You're Mad, Hurt, Scared, Frustrated, Insulted, Betrayed, or Desperate.* New York: HarperCollins Publishers, 2001

Lister, Pamela. *Stay in Lust Forever: 10 Secrets Every Couple Needs for a Long-Lasting Passionate Relationship.* New York: Sterling Publishing Co., Inc., 2001

Love, P. and J. Robinson. *Hot Monogamy: Essential Steps to More Passionate, Intimate Lovemaking.* Reprint Ed. New York: Plume, 1995

145

McCarthy, B.W. and E.J. McCarthy. *Rekindling Desire: A Step-byStep Program to Help Low-Sex and No-Sex Marriages.* Oxford: Routledge, 2003

Moore, Thomas. *The Care of the Soul: A Guide for Cultivating Depth and Sacredness in Everyday Life.* New York: HarperCollins Publishers, Inc., 1992

Moore, Thomas. *Soul Mates: Honoring the Mysteries of Love and Relationship.* New York: HarperCollins Publishers, Inc., 1994

Moore, Thomas. *The Soul of Sex: Cultivating Life as an Act of Love.* New York: HarperCollins Publishers, Inc., 1998

Moseley, Doug and Naomi. *Making Your Second Marriage a First-Class Success.* Rocklin, CA: Prima Publishing, 1998

Moseley, Doug and Naomi. *The Shadow Side of Intimate Relationships: What's Going on Behind the Scene.* Taos, NM: Moseley Method 2000
Ruiz, Don Miguel. *The Four Agreements: A Practical Guide to Personal Freedom (A Toltec Wisdom Book):* San Rafael, CA: Amber-Allen Publishing, 1997

Schnarch, David. *Passionate Marriage: Keeping Love and Intimacy Alive in Committed Relationships.* New York: Henry Holt and Company, LLC., 1997

Schnarch, David. *Resurrecting Sex: Resolving Sexual Problems and Rejuvenating Your Relationship.* New York: HarperCollins Publishers, 2002

Tannen, D. *You Just Don't Understand: Women and Men in Conversation.* New York: Harper Paperbacks, 2001

Weiner-Davis, M. *The Sex-Starved Marriage: Boosting Your Marriage Libido.* New York: Simon & Schuster, 2003

Weiner-Davis, M. *The Sex-Starved Wife: What to Do When He's Lost Desire.* New York: Simon @ Schuster, 2008

Zilbergeld, B. *The New Male Sexuality: The Truth About Men, Sex and Pleasure.* Rev. ed. New York- Bantam, 1999

Very Helpful Resources

Harville Hendrix-Getting the Love You Want: A Workshop for Couples was developed by Harville Hendrix, Ph.D, co-creator with his wife Helen LaKelly Hunt of Imago Relationship Therapy which is practiced in 30 countries. The workshop is offered by over 200 certified Imago workshop presenters internationally. The focus of the two day workshops is helping couples become "conscious partners." Couples are assisted towards this goal by learning a dialogue process that helps them dissolve their childhood issues and create a durable connection that heals and makes whole. Research on this workshop substantiates its power to transform not only couple's relationships but their lives as well. For a workshop near you, go to www.gettingtheloveyouwant.com.

Doug and Naomi Moseley- Group workshops for couples and individuals.

Workshops designed to help you access more of your emotional body which can lead to energizing your intimate relationships. Very Powerful!" www.intimacytraining.com. Facilities located in Taos, New Mexico.

David Schnarch and Ruth Morehouse- Weekend workshops and longer retreats for couples and individuals based on Schnarch's "Passionate Marriage" approach which emphasizes marriage as an area for personal growth and reaching your sexual potential

Marriage and Family Health Center in Evergreen, Colorado www.passionatemarriage.com

Judith Milburn- Anger Workshops   This small group weekend intensive provides a safe opportunity for people who are ready to deal with and express old, repressed or present day emotional material that is hampering their efforts to move forward. In this process, participants work individually with Judith so that you can go as deeply as you need/want to go.   Center   for   Conscious   Living,   Fountain   Valley,   CA www.judithmilburn.com

Sedona Method, Hale Dwoskin- facilitator   The Sedona Method is a unique, elegant, simple-to-master and very powerful tool that enables you to uncover your natural ability to "let go" of painful, unwanted, counterproductive feelings in the moment ... meaning before the negative feelings can do their damage to your inner peace, happiness, stability, relationships, goals and success.   Headquarters in Sedona, AZ. www.sedona.com